JESUS;
GOD OR MAN?

RICH KANYALI

Jesus; God or Man

ISBN: 978-1-5136-2711-3

Published by:
Rich Kanyali Ministries

P.O Box 243
Woodland Park Co 80866

RichKanyaliministries.com

Jesusgodorman@outlook.com

TABLE OF CONTENTS

Acknowledgments

I would like to thank my family members: my wife, Joanna, and my daughter, Shalom; my father, Patrick, and my mother, Ruth; my sisters, Lydia, Jackie and Hilda; my brothers, Nelson and Clinton. A big thank you to Clinton and Hilda for financially making this book a reality.

I would like also to give special thanks to the following people who have made a major positive impact on my life:

Mr. Andrew Wommack - It's an absolute privilege to serve at your ministry. I have learned a lot from you over the past nine years. You have taught me and inspired me so much. Your humility is very admirable. Your teaching quickened me to write this book. Thank you, so very much.

Pastor Greg Mohr (Director of Charis Bible College)

Pastor Lawson Perdue (Charis Christian Center)

Pastor Daniel Nkata (Uganda)

Pastor Charles Keega Mwirigi (India & Kenya)

Jonathan Semakula (Uganda)

Mr. Barry Bennett (Dean of students- Charis bible College)

Pastor/ Evangelist Steve Bartlett (Charis Bible College)

Instructor Daniel Bennett (Assistant Dean of Education- Charis Bible College)

Thank you all for impacting and changing my life—some of you at distance and some very closely. Thank you for your teaching and inspiration in my life.

DEDICATION

I would like to dedicate this book first and foremost to My Lord and Savior Jesus Christ, the one who loved me and gave Himself for me, the lover of my soul. Lord, I'm thankful and grateful for the good work you are doing in my life and for having called, anointed and separated me to the ministry. Thank You for touching my life to never be the same again, and thank You for the gift of teaching that You have placed on my life. I have decided to follow You, Lord Jesus, no turning back. I choose You, Lord Jesus—the one who first chose me.

I would also like to dedicate this book to my precious wife, Joanna, and my precious daughter, Shalom.

INTRODUCTION

This book is a product of detailed research over the last six years. It was primarily birthed from a conversation years ago with a few college friends from Yemen who challenged me on this topic. I went home, and I started studying. I picked up a daily devotional that was written by Andrew Wommack, and I stumbled upon a topic for that day that gave me the perfect direction in my research. I started to build on the direction that I received from this exceptional and seasoned teacher, and I took off from there.

I want to acknowledge the major part played by Andrew Wommack in shaping and awakening the teacher in me, which led me to research and start teaching others this simple, yet profound revelation.

"Jesus—God or man?" is a question that almost everyone has thought of at some point, Christian or non-Christian. It's a question worth much consideration and discussion. Let's take a deep journey through the Scriptures, examining what they have to say about Jesus. Was He truly God or was He truly man? Could He be both? Could He be 50% God and 50% man? Or could He be 100% God and 100% man? Which is it? What is the importance of knowing that Jesus *was* God? What difference does it make? I will be answering these questions in this book and giving detailed thoughts and scriptural evidence.

It's so vital to understand what the Scriptures teach and where you stand when it comes to the divinity of Jesus because if you don't stand for something, you can be led to believe anything or you will fall for anything. You have to know what the

Bible teaches, and be so grounded in it that no wave of doctrine will sway you into deception.

So buckle up, and sit tight as we take the journey into this profound revelation and answer all these questions.

CHAPTER ONE

Not Only a Man

Jesus was not just a good man sent from God or some kind of angel, a good master, a good teacher, and a good prophet. Jesus was and is God. This is the most important statement of the New Testament, and on this truth, hangs all other truths. Although most people do not pay attention to this truth, it is the most important truth the Bible presents.

Many people say that Jesus was a good man. Although that is true, it's not the whole truth. It's a partial truth.

If Jesus was only a man, then regardless of how good He was, His life could only provide a substitute for one other man. But it's well established in Scripture that Jesus' death was the payment for the sins of the whole world (1 John 2:2). This would have been impossible if Jesus was just a good man. He was not a mere man or else His sacrifice would not be worth the payment and substitution for all mankind. My point is that Jesus wasn't only a man.

If Jesus was just a man, then you are still in your sins, and no one can be saved. Of course that is not true. It would make all life hopeless and meaningless had Jesus been only a man. If Jesus was only a man, then His sacrifice was worthless to the whole world.

God the Father did not send a man less than Himself to pay for the sins of the entire human race. No mere man would qualify, no not one. Then what made Jesus qualify? Well, Jesus was God the Son, and that above all else made the difference. If Jesus' sacrifice was a perfect, complete, and blameless sacrifice, then it could not have been lesser than what God the Father would offer Himself. It had to be equal. What Jesus offered is equally what God the Father would have offered.

Since Jesus was God, His life was worth more than every human life since creation. Indeed, it was worth more than the sum total of the universe that He created. Jesus made an overpayment for our sins. He paid what we owed and beyond! What a Savior!

Let's assume you owed $10, 000 on your car. When Jesus decided to pay for it on your behalf, He paid a billion dollars. He paid more than enough.

Just believing that Jesus was another good man, a teacher but not God, is neither the gospel of Jesus nor the doctrine of Christ. It falls short of God's standard and expectation of your faith in Him, and that belief alone would not make Him the better sacrifice for you and would lead you into a search for more. Yet, there is nothing more. Jesus is all of it.

If all that God needed was just a good man to die for the sins of the entire world, then none would try to compete against Jesus. The truth is, God wasn't looking for just a good man to do this. He knew He was going to do this Himself because He was the only one capable, and He did it when he became a man named Jesus. Jesus *was* God incarnate.

God needed "God" to die to reconcile man back to Himself, and that left only God—Jesus in the qualification race. No man would qualify beyond merely being good, which none is.

Jesus was His own class. Although this God-Man, Jesus, came

dressed in a physical body, He was not merely another man like you and me. He was God manifest in the flesh—God incarnate (1 Tim. 3:16), Jesus humbled Himself and took upon Himself the form of a servant (Phil. 2:7).

This is one of the greatest truths in the Bible: Almighty God came to Earth in human form.

Now, that being said, we must not let the physical body of Jesus blind us to who He was and the fact that God became our friend.

It's important to know this truth (Jesus was and is God) because only then can you have true relationship with Him. I believe ignorance of this truth would mean you are having relationship with someone other than God or lesser than God—hence no salvation and eternal life.

Later in this book, we will go into greater detail and depth to expound on this truth.

The Son of God

A few years ago, I was speaking to a young Muslim man that I met on a train. I was speaking to him about Jesus. As we spoke, he asked me why Jesus is called the Son of God, yet God has no wife.

Well, my answer was very simple. I told the young man that "Son of God" doesn't mean God gave birth to a Son and called him Jesus. I told him that Jesus is not the Son of God in the sense that I am the son of Mr. Kanyali. There are three main names used by Jesus to identify Himself: The Son of man, the Son of David, and the Son of God.

Son of man was to identify Himself with humanity, *Son of David* with His Jewish heritage and *Son of God* with His divinity. Jesus was God and a Jewish man.

I told him that Jesus is God the Son. He is not lower than God, just as I am lower than my father. God is manifest in three persons: the Father, the Son, and the Holy Spirit. I told him the three are one, and they co-exist and are co-equal in everything (i.e. glory, power, splendor and majesty). Worshiping Jesus doesn't make God the Father or the Holy Spirit mad. Neither does praying to Jesus make God the Father or the Holy Spirit angry.

God the Father addresses Jesus as God. Jesus was a name given to God the Son when He took upon himself a physical body. The name *Jesus*, in its simplest form, means Savior or Messiah.

Equal with God

> *And therefore did the Jews persecute Jesus, and sought to slay him, because he had done these things on the Sabbath day. But Jesus answered them, My Father worketh hitherto, and I work. Therefore the Jews <u>sought the more</u> to kill him, because he not only had broken the Sabbath, but said also that God was his Father, making himself equal with God.* —John 5:16-18 (underline mine)

An examination of this verse speaks volumes on how the Jews and others understood what it meant for Jesus to call God His Father. All through Jesus' ministry and life, He addressed God as Father. As New Testament believers, we can now call God our Father as Matthew 6:9 teaches. This privilege was purchased for us by our union with and faith in Jesus as our Lord and Savior. However, it does not bestow divinity upon us.

Note that there were two reasons why the Jews wanted to kill Jesus. But of those two reasons, the most outstanding was that Jesus said that "God was His Father, making Himself equal with God."

They got more upset that Jesus had called God His Father. And it wasn't a question of *how can God have a Son?* It was about making Himself equal with God.

Wait a minute. What was wrong with Jesus calling God His Father? The Jews understood that Jesus, by calling God His Father, was making Himself equal to God. You see, it was obvious that no one had to tell them at this point what it meant. They already knew it. It's like they were studying or had learned this truth, which actually verifies and attests to Jesus' claim.

I think their reasoning about Jesus was true. Jesus was making Himself equal with God because **He was equal with God** (Phil. 2:6). He was God. He was equal with God the Father, and these people should not have sought to kill Him because He was speaking the truth. Jesus wouldn't have called God His Father if He wasn't equal to Him.

They were blinded by the humanity of Jesus (His physical body), but they understood what it meant to call God His Father.

I have spoken to hundreds of people about this striking truth, and it's like a light turned on inside of them. It clicked. And I pray that you will not be an exception.

CHAPTER TWO

Someone Is Wrong!

Many believers are either ignorant or blind and do not know what the Bible says. This is very dangerous because when someone comes along with a strange doctrine, they will fall for it. This brings me to a very destructive, non-Christian doctrine that is slowly creeping into the church.

In the1870s in Pennsylvania, the religious movement known today as the Jehovah's Witnesses, began as a Bible study led by Charles Taze Russell. Born on February 16, 1852, in Old Allegheny, Pennsylvania, Russell attended Allegheny City Congregational Church with his parents, who later changed his views of hell and expressed his doubts about eternal torment. In 1869, he abandoned his church and the Bible. In 1870, Russell attended a religious meeting led by a second Adventist speaker named Jonas Wendell, who taught that a person doesn't have a soul and that unbelievers are simply annihilated. This provided resolve to Russell's concerns about hell.

Two years later, Russell organized a Bible class to promote his views. In 1877, he met N. H. Barbour, a man who believed in the invisible return of Jesus. Russell, claiming to have come to the same conclusion, began to promote this view.

Russell published *The Watch Tower and Herald of Christ's Presence* in 1879 and founded the Zion Watch Tower Tract Society in 1884. By 1888, Russell's movement had grown to a leadership team of 50 people. Russell had published a series of books and was editing a growing magazine. In his writings, Russell predicted that God's judgment and the millennial age would occur by 1914. When his prophecies proved untrue, some "Russellites" left the fold. But because World War I began the same year, many thought Russell's prediction was close enough and that the prophecy would soon be fulfilled.

In modern times, this growing religious organization, now called Jehovah's Witnesses, has continued to expand nationally and internationally.

What do Jehovah's Witnesses believe? Although there are some similarities to Christianity, the movement has distorted fundamental beliefs regarding many key, biblical teachings.

For example: The Jehovah's Witnesses believe that Jesus was previously Michael the Archangel, reducing Jesus to the level of a created being. And as a result, they reject the deity of Jesus and the Christian belief in the Holy Trinity. They believe salvation comes through faith **plus** a list of works dictated by the Watch Tower organization, which contradicts what Scripture teaches. The Bible says,

> For by grace are ye saved through faith; and that
> not of yourselves: it is the gift of God: Not of
> works, lest any man should boast.
> —Ephesians 2:8-9

What this movement believes has deceived many and violates orthodox Christian beliefs. They changed and cherry picked the Holy Scriptures to develop their own "Bible" (New World Translation) in order to promote their occult doctrine. I guess they figured that using the existing, true scriptures would not further their agenda, ideas, and beliefs, so they decided to make their own. I believe it's a cult, with all due respect. It should be ex-posed with all its deception. This cult is very possessive, oppres-sive, and extremely controlling.

Further studies show that the similarities between the Je-hovah's Witnesses and the Masons are enormous—both clearly known as cults. So we see that what they proclaim to be truth is not the truth because they perverted the Word of God. This is a dead belief system and religion that considers itself to be a Chris-tian denomination yet it violates the very fundamental, Christian beliefs that the scriptures teach.

The word *Christian* comes from a Greek word, *Christianos*, which means *followers of Christ* (Strong's Concordance). It is used three times in the New Testament (Acts 11:26, Acts 26:28, 1 Peter 4:16). Christians are disciples, followers of, and believers in Jesus Christ as Lord and Savior, not the "Jesus" of the Jehovah's Witness-es, whom they believe was an archangel.

The "Jesus" of the Jehovah's Witnesses is not the same **Jesus** of the Holy Bible.

My point is that if Jesus was not God, then how can the Je-hovah's Witnesses, Hindus, Buddhists Christian Scientists, Latter Day Saints (founded by Joseph Smith in 1830) Christadelphians, Scientologists, Unification Church members, Oneness Pente-costals, Universalists, Mormons, Jesuits and (on and on the list goes) be saved? How can you then be saved? Can a *man* save the world? Can someone less than God atone for the sins of the world? This is a strong and logical question. If Jesus was only a man, how could He save you? After all, He is only a man. For Jesus to be your Savior, He's got to be God, since God is the only Savior (1 Tim.1:1, 2:3).

This cult (Jehovah's Witnesses) and many others were founded by **men**. And it is easy to figure out that this cult religion is neither *from* God nor *of* God.

You may be asking why I'm saying all these things about the Jehovah's Witnesses, among others. For one, I have had many encounters with Jehovah's Witnesses, but I'm using them as an example of all other religions and manmade organizations that have neglected or undermined the divinity of Jesus, yet claim relationship with Him. There are many religious cults out there that are damning people through deception.

My motive is not to inflict harm, but to expose and bring to light this deception that has damned many and is still doing so. At least, those who reject this will not be doing so out of ignorance but neglect. See, it's like a farmer who is going to plant a crop. He has to uproot all the weeds and cultivate the land to create a good opportunity for the seed to grow. Planting a crop in ground unprepared is not going to do any good for the crop.

> *Then the LORD put forth his hand, and touched my mouth. And the LORD said unto me, Behold, I have put my words in thy mouth. See, I have this day set thee over the nations and over the kingdoms, to root out, and to pull down, and to destroy, and to throw down, to build, and to plant.*
> — Jeremiah 1:9-10

When this word from God came to Jeremiah, he was to root out, pull down, to destroy and throw down *before* he could build and plant. I think God knew that it was important to clear the ground and destroy any kind of weeds before any building or planting could be done.

It's sad to say, even though Jehovah's Witnesses and others proclaim to be Christian, they do not believe what Scripture teaches, and they violate the basic teachings of Christianity, such as the divinity of Jesus, salvation, death, resurrection and the virgin birth.

In summary, the Jehovah's Witnesses movement, Jesuits, Mormons, Unification Church, etc. are not Christian denominations, and their core, theological beliefs set them apart as cults. Jehovah's Witnesses' views of God, Jesus, salvation, scriptures, and the afterlife are inconsistent with, incompatible to, and against Christianity.

A Muslim Guy

A few years ago, I met another Muslim guy who was from Yemen. We were going to the same college. He came to me, and said, "You Christians believe that Jesus is God, right?"

"Yes," I strongly replied.

He went on to say that Christianity and Islam are similar. "It's the same thing. There is no difference," he said.

"Jesus means *Isa* in *Islam*. Jesus is *Prophet Isa*," he said. I told him that Jesus is not Isa and that, although there are some similarities between Islam and Christianity, the MAIN thing is different. And since the main thing is different, anything else is of no importance, however similar it may be.

What's the main thing? Jesus—His divinity, death, resurrection, and the Holy Scriptures. If we can't agree on Jesus, who He was, what He said, what He came for, and what He achieved, then it is not important to agree on anything else. First things first!

Christianity is built on Jesus Christ as the foundation. Without Jesus, there would be no salvation for all mankind.

Anyway, he went on to say that everything the Quran says about Prophet Isa is similar to what we believe about Jesus. So he concluded that the prophet Isa in the Quran is the Jesus of the Bible. You see, the truth is that he believes *part* of what the Bible says about Jesus.

I began a study to learn about this Isa and who the Quran or Islam believes He was.

Fortunately, my discovery was thrilling. I discovered thousands of differences between the Quran Prophet Isa and Jesus of the Holy Bible. I understood that having similar names does not necessarily make people similar in any way, shape or form. You may have the same name as I do, but that doesn't make you me.

Jesus of the Bible vs. Isa the "Jesus" of the Quran

Example of differences:

Jesus	Who is He?	Isa
Virgin born; conceived by the Holy Spirit (Isaiah 7:14; Matthew 1:18-23; Luke 1:35)		Virgin born; created in womb of Mary by Allah; creation similar to Adam's (Surah 3:59, 19:20-22, 21:91)
Son of God (Matthew 3:17; John 10:30)		Son of Mary (called by this name 23 times in Islamic scriptures; for example: Surah 34:45)
		Allah is not a father and has no sons or daughters; to say so is *shirk*, the unpardonable sin (see Surah 19:88-92, 112:3).

Eternal (John 8:58, 17:5)	Created from dust, as Adam was (Surah 3:59)
Co-equal, co-eternal with the Father and the Holy Spirit (John 1:1-14; Colossians 1:15-20; Philippians 2:5-11; Hebrews 1:1-13)	Only a man, a prophet. It is shirk, the unpardonable sin, to ascribe deity to Jesus. Allah is not triune (Surah 4:171; 5:73, 116)
God (John 1:1, 10:30)	Not God (Surah 5:17, 72-3, 75) Jesus was an apostle of Allah (Surah 4:171); a messenger only (Surah 5:75, 19:30).
Greater than any man (Matthew 12:42)	A great prophet; not as great as Muhammad Jesus was a worshiper of Allah (Surah 3:51; 9:30).
Messiah/Christ (Matthew 16:16-17; John 20:31)	Messiah only to the Jews; will proclaim Islam and establish it on the earth at his return.
The way, truth, and the life (John 14:6)	Preached the truth (of Islam)
Savior of the world (Luke 2:11; John 4:42; Acts 5:31)	Prophet of Allah; human messenger
Sinless (2 Corinthians 5:21; Hebrews 4:15, 7:26; 1 Peter 2:22)	Righteous; obedient to Allah, as all prophets were (Surah 3:45, 49; 4:158)
Jesus **Who is He?** **Isa**	
Became flesh, retaining His deity; adding humanity (John 1:14)	Was only flesh, created from dust by Allah (Surah 3:59)
Called God His Father (John 5:18, 8:54, 20:17)	Called Allah his Lord and worshipped him (Surah 5:75)
Performed miracles to demonstrate His authority as Messiah and to provide a foretaste of the kingdom of heaven (John 2:11; Acts 2:22)	Performed miracles as "signs from the Lord" (Surah 3:49, 5:110)

Died on the cross for our sins (1 Corinthians 15:3; 2 Corinthians 5:21)	Did not die on the cross; Opinions vary as to what happened to him (he hid while one of his companions died in his place; Allah made Judas Iscariot to look like Jesus and take his place; Simon of Cyrene took Jesus' place); Atonement for sins not necessary (Surah 17:15, 35:18)
Rose physically from the dead (Matthew 12:38-40; Romans 1:4; 1 Corinthians 15:4-8; 1 Peter 1:18-21)	Did not die
Ascended into heaven after His resurrection and is seated at the Father's right hand (Matthew 26:64; Mark 16:19; Acts 7:55-56)	Called into heaven by Allah at the time Christians say he was crucified; Opinions vary as to whether he remains in heaven today or was sent back to earth, where he died a natural death.
Will return physically and visibly one day to establish His earthly kingdom (Matthew 24:30-31; Revelation 19:11-21)	Will return one day to proclaim Islam and establish Islam on earth; Will defeat Antichrist, kill all pigs, break all crosses, and establish 1,000 years of righteousness; Some expound on this and say he will then die and be buried beside Muhammad.
Jesus **What difference does it make?** **Isa**	
Sin is humanity's problem and results in spiritual and physical death (Romans 3:10, 3:23, 5:12, 6:23)	People are not fallen by nature. Sin is not humanity's problem; ignorance of the teachings of Islam is the problem
Christ's finished work on the cross provides forgiveness of sin and eternal life by God's grace through faith (John 3:16, 5:24; Romans 4:4-5; Ephesians 2:8-9; Titus 3:5-7).	Allah would never let his prophet die in such a way. Forgiveness of sins and eternal life are achieved by submitting to Allah and performing good deeds; atonement is not needed (Surah 11:114, 17:15, 35:18).

Jesus is the only way of salvation (John 14:6; Romans 3:24-26).	Jesus was only a man—a good man, a prophet, and a worshiper of Allah (Surah 3:51, 19:30).
Salvation is offered freely to all (Romans 10:13).	Allah forgives and punishes whom he pleases; from mankind's perspective, our eternal destiny is fatalistically determined (Surah 11:114).
Believers are eternally secure, based on the promise of God to save us and the power of God to keep us saved (John 5:24, 10:28; 1 Peter 1:3-5).	Jihad is the only eternal security (Surah 3:157).
God deals graciously with people; worship is never forced (Matthew 11:28-30).	Worship may be forced upon people (Surah 2:193, 9:29).

This table was compiled with reference to Rob Phillip of *OnceDelivered.net*.

Although there are certain, supposed similarities between the Prophet Isa of Islam and Jesus of the Bible, they are two different people as clearly seen in the Bible and the Quran. **So, these two cannot be the same person.**

Many who are not familiar with this truth end up believing that these two are the same, which is a wrong conclusion that will lead Christians into Islam. After my research, I was fully equipped to challenge this fallacy, and I dismissed any sort of similarity.

If we cannot agree on Jesus, we cannot agree on salvation, God, etc.

Once more, I would like to kill a few more sacred cows.

CHAPTER THREE

Mary, the Mother of Jesus

Who was Mary? Mary was the virgin girl who was espoused to Joseph. An angel appeared to her and announced the good tidings, and said, "...Hail thou art highly favored, the Lord is with thee. Blessed are thou among women" (Luke 1:28).

According to Mark 3:35, "Whosoever shall do the will of God: (which is to believe on Jesus Christ) the same is my brother, and my sister, and my mother" (parentheses mine).

Mary was highly favored. Favor is something you do not deserve. You don't earn it as a wage. It's free, underserved, and unmerited. She did not deserve to be chosen by God. That's why scriptures say she was favored. Although it was a great honor for her to be the mother of the Messiah or the woman God used to give Jesus a human body, it is idolatry to elevate Mary to a place above other humans because she gave birth to the Messiah. It's equally wrong to elevate Mary to divinity. Mary was not divine. She was not God. She was a mere human like you and me. Luke 1:47 says that she rejoiced in God, her Savior. So, if she had to have a savior, then she wasn't sinless; she wasn't divine. Mary needed a savior just like all of us. That's why she rejoiced in God, her Savior.

There is one other thing to notice in Scripture. No one ever worshipped Mary. Do you know why? Because they knew she wasn't God manifest in the flesh, and therefore, she didn't qualify for worship. No single person ever did, not the disciples and not Mary. Only Jesus the Son of God qualified.

Mary never hung on the cross for your sins. She was no Messiah! She did not die for anyone's sins. Why would she? She had her own sins just like all of us? She has never born our griefs and carried our sorrows. She was never wounded for our transgressions, nor bruised for our iniquities. She was never chastised for our peace, and she took no stripes for us to be healed.

Just as every believer in Jesus is highly favored, so was she. Actually, some have been led to believe that because she was the Mother of Jesus, it puts her in a separate higher class; yet that is not true. As a matter of fact, it was never intended, and scripture never instructs us to pray to Mary, nor asks her to pray for us. Romans 8:26-27 says that the Holy Spirit makes intercession for us. Notice, it does not say Mary makes intercession for us!

It's the traditions of men that have elevated her to a place where people think she can answer prayers or God will hear when she prays. I don't know where people get these strange, weird beliefs, but they are not scriptural. That is not what God's Word teaches.

One of the main reasons people are in error and powerless is because they do not know the Holy Scriptures (Mk. 12:24).

In Luke 11:28, Jesus told a woman who was praising Mary for being His mother that those who keep God's Word are more blessed than Mary. What a statement! It's loaded, speaks volumes, and it's from the mouth of Jesus.

If Mary was that big of a deal, then the Scriptures would have said volumes about her. Now, I'm not trying to diminish her role in the birth of Jesus; I am only trying to say what she was and is not. Sometimes I wonder what Mary would be thinking in relation to all these elevations if she were alive today. I believe that she would disagree with what some people are doing.

Jesus was the only man who never had any sin in His life. He never sinned (2 Cor. 5:21; Heb. 4:15, 7:26; 1 Pet. 2:22). Jesus was able to pay for our sins because He was God and the Sacrificial Lamb. He had no sins of His own to pay for. Hallelujah!

My point is that Mary was another human being, a sinner who needed a Savoir, just like you and me. Actually, Luke 1:47 really portrays what she thought of herself, not what people thought about her.

Mary would be shocked to see what people are doing today regarding who they believe she is. I personally think that Mary would be crying. She would cry because people have elevated her to a place she does not belong. She would cry because some people worship her erroneously. She would cry because people have missed the Savior—Jesus Christ and have focused on His mother, which was never commanded nor intended. She would cry because sincere people are sincerely wrong and are doomed unless they repent. She would cry because people do not even know what God's Word teaches and are caught up in religious customs and the traditions of men. The Bible says, "My people are destroyed for lack of knowledge..." (Hosea 4:6).

She would cry because people have made images in direct opposition to God's Word to never make any graven images.

Thou shalt not make unto thee any graven image, or any likeness of anything that is in heaven above, or that is in the earth beneath, or that is in the wa-ter under the earth: Thou shalt not bow down thy-

self to them, nor serve them: for I the LORD thy
God am a jealous God, visiting the iniquity of the
fathers upon the children unto the third and fourth
generation of them that hate me.
—Exodus 20:4-5

She would also cry because people think she is something she really isn't. She is not even the image they always worship, which is the image of a Babylonian queen named Semiramis.

Mary has her place, but it's not the place where many have put her. I am trying to show you her place.

Now, let me move on. There are many other people exalted to deity by some—people such as the Pope, Our Lady of Guadalupe (Queen of Mexico), Saints and many occult leaders.

Over the years, many have been deceitfully elevated to a degree of divinity claiming to be superior to other human beings, and hence called "God." The truth is, these people are nobodies. They are not God. Further study of Scripture reveals that no man is divine or God. All these people who claim divinity are manipulative liars. They violate what the Scriptures teach. They deserve no worship because they aren't God. Worship belongs to and is reserved for God alone. It's important to put all these people in the *place* where they belong—mere humans who are sinners by nature and in need of a savior (Jesus) just like the rest of us.

Hear the truth, so the truth can make you free (John 8:23-32). If I have stepped on your toes, Jesus will heal them. But it is good news for you that God would become a man to die for the sins of the entire human race, so we would be reconciled to God and have a relationship with Him. His motivation was love. He loves you, and if you think He stopped loving you at some point, I want to remind you that He hasn't.

You cannot put God on the same level as man or another god and still put faith in Him to be your Savior. It's impossible because you would then be putting faith in someone lesser than God, and sadly, that cannot and will not save you. You can't be born again that way. We need to exalt God to His place, and put all others in their respective places—where they belong. Jesus is the One True God and Eternal Life (1 John 5:20).

Furthermore, Jesus is the Son of God in that He is the manifestation of God in the flesh (John 1:1, 14). John 1:1 says, "In the beginning was the Word, and the Word was with God, and the Word was God."

This Word that was in the beginning was with God and was God. Who is this Word? Jesus is this Word. Jesus was and is the Word spoken of here. John 1:14 says "And the Word was made flesh, and dwelt among us, and we beheld his glory…." This is saying that Jesus (God and the Word) became human (flesh) and dwelt or lived among us.

The conclusion to be drawn from this scripture is that Jesus is the Son of God. He was God, who later went on to become a human being. Jesus was God, and it's that clear.

Jesus Is God

It's interesting to understand what Satan knew about Jesus.

In Matthew chapter 4, we see a series of temptations from Satan toward Jesus. Some people have been led to think that Satan was tempting Jesus to turn the stone into bread because he was hungry. They think the temptation was all about Jesus performing a miracle of turning the stone into bread, but that is not true. The temptation was to get Jesus to **doubt** who He was. That's why two of the temptations started by saying, "If thou be the Son of God." Jesus was God incarnate (1 Tim. 3:16), but He humbled Himself, took upon Himself the form of a servant, and became a man (Phil. 2:6-8). The human part of Jesus was capable of doubting who He was or the tempter wouldn't have used this approach.

Satan, the tempter, was trying to get Jesus to doubt that He was God and have Him perform a miracle to prove His identity, which would only have revealed his doubt or unbelief. That would have been sin, and it would have disqualified Him. Praise God, He didn't yield! Otherwise, it would have taken away all our hope. Jesus is the Hope of the World.

Now let's look at verse 7 of Matthew 4. "Jesus said unto him, it is written again, thou shalt not tempt the Lord thy God."

Who was Satan tempting here? Jesus, right? Right. Yet, Jesus told Satan "thou shalt not tempt the Lord thy God." Who was Jesus referring to, since the conversation was only between the two of them? Who was Jesus referring to when He said "the Lord thy God?" The answer is very clear. Jesus was referring to Himself. Jesus called Himself *the Lord thy God* right in front of Satan. Jesus claimed His deity right before Satan's eyes, and Satan never challenged His claim. Why didn't Satan object? The answer is very simple. I believe that Satan knew that Jesus was God. If Jesus was not God, then Satan would've strongly objected. If Jesus had been lying, Satan would have expressed some kind of disapproval. He would've spoken up against Jesus' claim. But Satan's lack of objection to who Jesus was or claimed to be means that he knew that Jesus was God and wasn't lying.

Again in verse 10 of Matthew 4, after Satan told Jesus to worship him, Jesus responded in verse 10 saying "…Get thee hence, Satan: for it is written, Thou shalt worship the Lord thy God, and him only shalt thou serve."

Jesus objected to Satan's demands for worship and told him that he (Satan) was the one who should worship Jesus—the Lord thy God.

Why did Jesus object to Satan's demands? Simple, it's because Satan was not God and did not deserve any worship whatsoever.

This is the second time in this passage that Jesus declares His deity before Satan, yet His enemy did not disagree because He knew that Jesus was God.

Jesus reminded Satan that He wasn't merely a man, He was God. Hallelujah! He is reminding you too! And in this specific verse, Jesus says that only God is worthy of worship, and He told Satan to only worship God. It was Satan who was supposed to worship Jesus (God). Satan is a pervert. He perverts every order that God sets up.

It's critical to see and understand Satan's thinking in relation to this exchange with Jesus. It's equally amazing to understand that Satan (the tempter) knew, understood, and agreed with Jesus' statements of who He was.

It's also sad to say that many people don't know any better than Satan (the devil). They disagree with who Jesus said He was, and yet they consider themselves smart. In this case, Satan knew better and is *"smarter"* than those who disagree.

The Rich, Young Ruler

Mark 10:17-20 talks about a rich, young ruler who came running to Jesus, knelt down, and asked Him, "Good Master, what shall I do that I may inherit eternal life?"

Publicly, this young man looked good, but his heart held something different. He looked good as he ran and knelt before Jesus. Jesus was God, and was able to look beyond this man's outward display straight to his heart (1 Sam. 16:7). As He looked in his heart, He knew that this man wasn't willing to elevate Him to His rightful place as God. The young ruler's heart wasn't right, neither was his question. Because he believed he had kept all the commandments, which wasn't even true, he asked Jesus, "Good Master, what shall I **do** to inherit eternal life? He believed that eternal life had to be **earned**. He thought he had to perform or do certain things to produce, earn or receive eternal life.

You can't earn your way to God. No way! It's not what we do for God that produces eternal life (a relationship with God the Father through Jesus), but what Jesus has done for us. Eternal life is a gift to be received, not a wage to be earned (Eph.2:8-9; Rom. 10:9-10; Mk. 16:16; John 1:12; Acts 16:30-31). This man was trying to earn eternal life. Not good, and definitely not smart!

In Mark 10, verse 18, Jesus asks him, "...Why callest me good? There is none good but one, that is, God."

In other words, Jesus was saying, *either call me God, since you said I am good, or don't call me good.* Jesus was saying that God alone is good, and if you recognize that I am good, why don't you call me God? After all, I am.

The young man recognized Jesus just as a good man, but not as God, just as many people today believe that he was just a good man, an angel or a second-place god. Jesus wanted to get him to put total faith in Him, not just a partial faith.

My friend, just as we see in this passage, calling Jesus a good man, a prophet, a teacher or a leader is not enough. We must acknowledge and recognize Him as God.

The young man needed to acknowledge Jesus as God, but Mark 10:20 shows that he didn't. No man can earn God's salvation. You can't live 'good enough' to earn it. You can only get it as a gift—free. Once you try to earn it, it ceases to be a gift. And as a matter of fact, you *can't* earn it. It's just impossible.

"And he answered and said unto Him, Master, ..." We see here that the young ruler dropped **good** from **good Master**, and he referred to Jesus just as **Master**. Remember, Jesus had told him to either call Him God or quit calling Him good. In Mark 10:18 and here in verse 20, he dropped the good and just called Jesus Master. Amazing! This reveals the heart of the young man and his religious displays of running and kneeling. He wasn't willing to worship Jesus as God.

Many people today are just like this rich, young ruler. They make all these religious displays, but in their hearts, Jesus is not given His rightful place. He is still a **good master** to some, and to others, He is **master**—but not God.

Jesus desires you to relate to Him as He is—God. God is good. If Jesus is good, you might as well believe, and call Him who He truly is—God. Jesus will not accept anything less than God. I mean, why should He? He was God, and He is God. Amen!

This scripture reveals that Jesus was God and that people know it in their hearts, but reject it. If Jesus is God, then you can be saved and have a personal relationship with Him, but if He is not God, then you are lost forever because you can't have a relationship with another human being that produces salvation and eternal life. Jesus is Lord and God. Hallelujah!

Chapter Four

Jesus before the High Priest

It's even far more interesting and exciting to know that Jesus knew He was God. Even in times of pressure, He did not budge, bend, nor bow. He stood by the truth when asked by the high priest if He was the Son of God, and He openly admitted that He was (God manifest in the flesh). For this, He was accused of blasphemy (Matt. 26:64-66).

Jesus had earlier claimed to be equal with God—the Son of God (John 5:18), and the high priest, understanding what it meant for Him to claim to be the Son of God, responded by tearing his robes because Jesus, at the highest level, meant that He was God.

In John 19:7, the Jews insisted that Jesus must die for claiming deity. It is so informative to see that even if these men wanted to kill Jesus for claiming to be God the Son, He did not change His claim. He didn't apologize for any of His statements because he was claiming what was rightfully His—deity. He was God, manifest in the flesh, and had nothing of which to repent.

Today, very few people would be willing to die for what they believe, but Jesus surely was, setting an example for you and me.

One main lesson to learn from this trial of Jesus is never to budge, bend or bow if you know you are doing the right thing. It's exciting and educational to know that the high priest and the Jews knew what it meant for Jesus to call Himself the Son of God, equal with God or God in the flesh.

Mocking Jesus

And the soldiers led him away into the hall, called Praetorium; and they call together the whole band. And they clothed him with purple, and plaited a crown of thorns, and put it about his head, And began to salute him, Hail, King of the Jews! And they smote him on the head with a reed, and did spit upon him, and bowing their knees worshipped him. And when they had mocked him, they took off the purple from him, and put his own clothes on him, and led him out to crucify him.

—Mark 15:16-20

This was not pure worship, obviously. It was mockery. But think about this: If Jesus hadn't claimed deity or to be the Christ, these soldiers wouldn't have mocked Him through worship. Why worship and not something else? Why didn't they mock him as a carpenter, cattle keeper or anything else? I really believe that by mocking Him through worship, they were making a certain point unaware—that God alone deserves worship, and they were ignoring that Jesus was God and was worshipped many times previously. As mentioned earlier, Jesus had been worshipped before by many others.

It's important to note that at no time did Jesus reject being called the Christ nor rebuke anyone. He actually blessed Peter (Matt. 16:17) for recognizing this.

Jesus in the Garden of Gethsemane

(Jesus was no less than God on earth, praying to the Father.)

So, if Jesus was God, how could He pray to God? Was Jesus praying to Himself?

It's important to understand that Jesus, as God on earth, praying to God the Father in heaven, demonstrates a unity between the two. The eternal Father and the eternal Son had an eternal relationship before Jesus took upon Himself the form of a man. And that exclusive unity between them never ceased when He came to the earth. He Jesus did not become God the Son when He was born in Bethlehem. He has always been the Son of God from eternity past, still is God the Son, and always will be. As a matter of fact, in Luke 2:11, the angel called Jesus "Saviour, Christ the Lord." That clearly shows that even at birth Jesus was Lord—God.

Jesus, God the Father, and the Holy Spirit have always existed, not as three Gods, but one God, existing or expressed in three persons. That's why Jesus claimed deity—because He was God (John 10:30). The Father, the Son, and the Holy Spirit are three co-equal persons existing as God—singular.

All that being said, it's important to remember that although Jesus was God, He was a man. Let me put it this way; He was God—Man. Jesus was so human that people struggled to accept that He was God. They looked at Him and saw nothing physically special. Isaiah 53:2 says that "… he hath no form nor comeliness; and when we shall see him, there is no beauty that we should desire him."

He wasn't one of those "beautiful people." This doesn't necessarily mean He was ugly, but He definitely wasn't physically special. Physically, He wasn't one of those handsome, flashy, six-pack-ab people everyone admires, wants to be around and be seen with, and receive recognition from. He was just plain and ordinary. If you had seen Him walk the earth, you wouldn't have been so impressed. There was nothing physically special about Him.

Jesus walked, ate, laughed, went to the bathroom, got dirty, got tired, slept, got angry, got hungry, and on and on the list goes. Jesus became like we are. Seeing all this about Jesus made it hard to believe this was God! Why? Because He looked so human that His physical being blinded some men to His spiritual being. The Spirit of Jesus was wall to wall God. On the *spiritual level*, Jesus was God, and on the *physical level*, He was a man. He was 100% God and 100% man. He wasn't 50/50.

Prior to becoming a man, Jesus, who was Almighty God, full of glory and majesty and honor, laid aside His glory and became a man. He took upon Himself the form of a servant and was made in the likeness of men. Jesus was still God when He became a man. Yet He concealed His divinity in a physical body. Thereby, the King became a servant!

CHAPTER FIVE

The Very Nature of God

Who being in the form of God, thought it not rob-
bery to be equal with God: but made himself of
no reputation, and took upon Him the form of
a servant, and was made in the likeness of men.
                                        —Philippians 2:6-7

The word *"form"* is the word for *"nature."* The NIV says that Jesus was "the very nature of God."

The Message Bible says, "...he set aside the privileges of deity and took on the status of a slave, became human! Having become human, he stayed human."

This scripture goes on to prove that Jesus was God and that He did not think it was robbery or unjust to be equal with God. Jesus was equal with God, and He knew it. He didn't think He was robbing or stealing from God by being equal with Him. Yet even with that level of knowledge, He said, "I will become a servant. I will limit and confine myself in a physical body." Amazing! Therefore, God became a man who was called Jesus.

Understanding that He was not in His full glory as God on earth because of the limitations of a physical body, Jesus had to depend on the Father for guidance, fellowship, and communion. They were united to the point that one could not operate independent of the other (See Gen. 1:26, "Let *Us* make man in *Our* own image...." [emphasis mine])

So Jesus, in His all earthly ministry, had to depend on God the Father and the Holy Spirit (Acts 5:4), as we can also see in Acts 10:38.

That explains why Jesus, God and man at the same time, had to pray to God the Father. He had limitations because He had a physical body and needed to depend on the Father, who had sent Him. For example, Jesus was God and man, yet He had to be physically taught how to speak, walk, dress, etc. He had to learn all the basic things that you and I have learned. He increased in favor and wisdom (Luke 2:52).

Jesus emotionally and physically felt pain, intense pain; the cross wasn't some game that Jesus would just easily endure. All the sin of the entire human race was carried by Him. It was all placed on Him. It was such a painful experience that it can't be portrayed on TV and fully understood. It takes a revelation from the Holy Spirit. A movie could only do so much.

The Bible actually says that He *became* sin. "He that knew no sin, became sin that you might be made the righteousness of God" (2 Cor. 5:21). He took your sins and gave you His righteousness, benefits and privileges. There was an exchange. He took all your mess and gave you His goodness.

Finally, Jesus praying to the Father doesn't necessarily mean that He was petitioning God for something. Most people think prayer is nothing but petitioning (asking for something).Prayer is communion with God above all else. Sometimes this communion may involve asking or petitioning, but it doesn't always have to. You can pray without asking. It's probable that Jesus was praying, yet not asking.

What Did God the Father Say about Jesus?

It's one thing for me and for others to say Jesus was and is God, but it's an even greater testimony to see God the Father calling Jesus God! This is such a powerful ingredient to all we have seen because it continues to confirm the things I have said thus far in this book.

A close look at Hebrews 1:1-8 speaks volumes to the truth that Jesus was God. To start with, Hebrews 1:3 says, "Who being the brightness of his glory, and the express image of his person...."

This scripture says that Jesus is the brightness of His (God the Father's) glory. Isaiah 42:8 says that the Lord will not share His glory with another. Therefore, Jesus is the Lord since He is the brightness of God the Father's glory. Jesus = Brightness of the Father's Glory. Romans 3:23 calls Jesus "the glory of God." This is more proof of Jesus' deity.

"...and the express image of His person." Hebrews 1:3 continues to say that Jesus was the express image of God the Father. The term *express image* means an **exact copy**. Wow! Jesus was exactly like the Father. He was an exact copy. He perfectly represented God to us. If we look at Jesus, we are looking at God the Father (John 14:9). If you see Jesus, you don't need to see the Father. You have already seen Him. Now, some might be thinking of the physical part of Jesus. In His Spirit, He was an exact copy of God the Father, and His works and actions here on earth were a perfect picture and representation of the Father.

Hebrews 1:6 goes on to say "...and let the angels of God worship him." God commanded all the angels to worship Jesus. Notice, not just a few of the angels, but **all** of the angels. So if all

JESUS; GOD OR MAN?

worship is reserved for God alone (Isa. 42:8), why would God the Father command all the angels to worship Jesus if He was not God or was inferior? It's clear that God the Father knew that Jesus was who He claimed to be and so commanded the angels to worship Him. There is no one in the Scriptures that God ever commanded to be worshipped, except Jesus—God the Son. This proves that Jesus was God and deserved worship (Psa. 45:11, 95:6).

God would not have all the angels worship someone inferior to Him. The person that God commands to be worshipped has to be God or equal to Him. Jesus was equal to God. He wasn't inferior. He was God in a physical body, and He deserved worship, even by all the angels, just as the Father. Let me also say that the angels would not have worshipped an equal, only one who was greater. Jesus was greater—indeed, far greater.

Thy Throne, O God

> But unto the Son he (God the Father) saith, thy throne, O God is forever and ever: a sceptre of righteousness, is the sceptre of thy kingdom.
> —Hebrews 1:8 (parentheses mine)

I love this scripture. It speaks volumes. God the Father is referring to Jesus as God. This is more conclusive proof of the deity of the Lord Jesus Christ. It is proof that Jesus was and is God, not a god, but GOD.

Wait a minute. God called Jesus God. Selah. Why? It's only because Jesus was and is God. God would not have called Jesus God if he weren't God. This would have been a complete lie. It is well established in Scripture that God cannot lie—FULLSTOP. Well, I'm glad He called Jesus God because this is the greatest proof, above all the others I've been pouring out so far. Jesus was and still is God, not just a mere man.

After God the Father commanded all the angels to worship Jesus, He went on to call Jesus *God*. This is a truth that cannot be ignored. It's pivotal. Hallelujah! Jesus was God. Jesus *is* Lord God Almighty.

He also said that His throne is forever and ever. In other words, only the throne of God is everlasting. God's throne is forever and ever.

CHAPTER SIX

Old Testament and prophecies Testify Jesus Was God

For unto us a child is born, unto us a Son is given; and the government shall be upon his shoulder and his name shall be called Wonderful, Counselor, The mighty God, The everlasting Father, the prince of peace.

—Isaiah 9:6

This is one of the most powerful scriptures in the Old Testament. God spoke through the prophet Isaiah what was going to happen in the future. Jesus was to be born to us, and His name was to be Wonderful, Counselor, the mighty God, the everlasting Father, the prince of peace. God, through the prophet Isaiah, called Jesus *"the* mighty God." The word *"the"* is a definite article. It is referring to *"only one person,"* excluding anyone else. It is clear that this is speaking about one person. If God the Father is *the mighty God*, Jesus is equally *the mighty God*. Furthermore, God continued on to call Jesus "The everlasting Father." This proves the point that Jesus was and is equal to the Father and that they are one (John 5:18; 10:30). It also further verifies the truth that when we see Jesus, we have seen the Father (John 14:9).

Jesus and God Used Interchangeably

In the following scriptures, you will see that Jesus and God are used interchangeably or as a substitute for each other, revealing a similarity and an additional meaning and explanation.

... unto me (God) every knee shall bow....
                    —Isaiah 45:23 (parentheses mine)

That at the name of Jesus (God) every knee should bow....
                    —Philippians 2:10 (parentheses mine)

Jesus and God are used interchangeably, showing their unity.

"In the beginning God created the heaven and the earth" (Gen. 1:1). Jesus was the Creator (Isa. 44:24). John 1:1-3 says Jesus was the Creator. Colossians 1:16-17 says Jesus created all things.

All the above scriptures from different books talk about creation and say that God created the heavens and the earth. But then they go on to say that Jesus is the creator. The conclusion would be that Jesus is God.

Genesis 17:1 says, "...I am the Almighty God...." Isaiah 9:6 says Jesus is the mighty God, and Revelation 1:7-8 says Jesus is the Almighty God. Therefore, Jesus was and still is God. He is the Almighty God.

In Exodus 3:14, "I am" was God. John 8:58 says Jesus is the "I am." If God was the "I am," and Jesus was the "I am," it means Jesus—the I am—was God. *Jesus = God = I am.*

Isaiah 43:15 says, "I am the Lord, your Holy One, the creator of Israel, your King." Acts 3:14 says Jesus was the Holy One.

Isaiah 44:6 says the First and the Last was God. Revelation 22:13 says Jesus is the First and the Last.

Isaiah 40:3 says, "The voice of him that crieth in the wilderness, Prepare ye the way of the LORD, make straight in the desert a highway for our God."

It's pretty very clear that this instruction from God was to John the Baptist, the forerunner of Jesus. This was the command: to prepare the way for the coming of Jesus. John the Baptist knew this command, and he applied it to himself in John 1:23. It's important to recognize that this passage refers to Jesus as **God**. It says "Prepare ye the way of the Lord, make straight in the desert a highway for our **GOD**." So this is another scripture that reveals that Jesus was God. What a proof!

Putting all these pieces of the puzzle together, you will find that scriptures comment on scriptures, revealing that Jesus was and is God. The Bible is its own commentary. If you keep reading and studying, you will see that. One book says something, and another book confirms it. All the above scriptures reveal the truth that Jesus was God. This overwhelming evidence in Scripture cannot be ignored.

Old Testament prophecy fulfillment is one of the greatest arguments of who Jesus was. This is one of most convincing arguments that Jesus was the Christ. It's important to note that all the things that happened to Jesus were prophesied hundreds of years before, and He perfectly fulfilled them.

In Acts chapter 2, as Peter preached to the people under the inspiration of the Holy Ghost, he quoted Old Testament scriptures to prove to them that Jesus was indeed the Messiah. To someone sincerely seeking the truth, this is an irresistible argument.

The way these scriptures played out, no one can argue with the truth that Jesus was and is God. The fulfillment of these scriptures cannot be a coincidence. There are hundreds and some-times thousands of years between when they were prophesied and when they were fulfilled.

Here are some of the Old Testament prophecies concerning His death and their New Testament fulfillment.

O.T. REFERENCE	PROPHECY	N.T. FULFILLMENT
Genesis 3:15	Victory over Satan	Colossians 2:15
Numbers 21:9	Type of serpent	John 3:14-15
Psalms 16: 10	The Messiah would not see corruption	Acts 2:27, 31; 13:35
Psalms 22:1	Christ forsaken	Matthew 27:46; Mark 15:34
Psalms 22:7-8	Messiah mocked and ridiculed	Luke 23:35
Psalms 22:16	Piercing of His hands and feet	Mark 15:25; Luke 23:33; John 19:37; 20:25
Psalms 22:18	Parting His garments and casting lots for them	Luke 23:34; John 19:23-24
Psalms 34:20	Not one bone broken	John 19:36
Psalms 35:11	Accused falsely	Mark 14:57-58
Psalms 35:19	Hated without a cause	John 15:24-25
Psalms 41:9	Betrayed by a close associate	Luke 22:47-48
Psalms 49:15	His resurrection	Mark 16:6-7
Psalms 68:18	His ascension to God's right hand	Mark 16:19; Ephesians 4:8
Psalms 69:21	Given vinegar to drink in His thirst	Matthew 27:34, 48; Mark 15:36; John 19:29
Psalms 109:25	They reviled Him, wagging their heads	Matthew 27:39

Isaiah 50:6	They spit in His face	Matthew 26:67
Isaiah 50:6	The Messiah scourged	Matthew 27:26
Isaiah 52:14	Lost human appearance by physical mistreatment	Matthew 27:26; Mark 15:15
Isaiah 52:15	Gentiles shall receive spiritual cleansing	Hebrews 1:3
Isaiah 53:3	He was despised and rejected of men	John 1:10-11
Isaiah 53:4	He bore our sickness	Matthew 8:16-17
Isaiah 53:5-6	He was wounded for our transgressions	Romans 4:25; 1 Peter 3:18
Isaiah 53:7	He opened not His mouth	Matthew 26:63; 27:12, 14; Mark 15:5; 1 Peter 2:23
Isaiah 53:9	He was buried with the rich	Matthew 27:57-58, 60
Isaiah 53:11	He shall justify many	Romans 3:26, 5:19
Isaiah 53:12	He was numbered with the transgressors	Mark 15:28; Luke 22:37
Isaiah 53:12	He was crucified with criminals	Mark 15:27-28
Jonah 1:17	The sign of the prophet Jonah	Matthew 12:40; 16:4
Micah 5:1	Smitten with the rod upon the cheek	Matthew 27:30
Zechariah 11:12	He was betrayed for thirty pieces of silver	Matthew 26:15
Zechariah 11:13	The betrayal money was used to buy the potter's field	Matthew 27:5-10
Zechariah 13:7	The shepherd is smitten and the flock is scattered	Matthew 26:31; Mark 14:27

(Chart compiled as cited in *Christian Philosophy* by Andrew Wommack.)

God with Us

Behold, a virgin shall be with child, and shall bring forth a son, and they shall call his name Emmanuel, which being interpreted is, God with us.
                                        —Matthew 1:23

During the Christmas season, we tend to read this passage often, right? Right. Have you ever stopped and thought about what the name *Emmanuel* means, and why Jesus was to be called Emmanuel?

It's important to understand why Jesus was to be called Emmanuel. Why not some other name? The meaning of that name is very significant. It means *God with Us*. **Jesus was God who came to be with us**, and his name *Emmanuel* was saying the very same thing. Way before Jesus was born, the instruction to His parents was to call Him Emmanuel, which means God with us. Surely, Jesus was God with Us. Yes, God. Even at birth, Jesus was God.

This passage helps continue to build the case that Jesus was and is God. Indeed, God came to be with us.

Death of the Apostles

Over the years, we have seen that people are ready to die for what they believe. The disciples of Jesus were not an exception.

Let's examine a few of them and what they died for or died believing. Many people today would love to have lived in Jesus' day, to have seen Him, to have walked with Him and to have seen all the miracles He did.

It's interesting to discover that the disciples of Jesus were later challenged for pretty much all that they believed. Their beliefs were put to the test, and many of them died as a result. But regardless of the consequences, they stood strong, and they never gave up. They never denied what they believed for fear of losing their lives. Few people today could match or measure up to the standard they set. They knew Jesus like no one else in their day. These guys lived with Him; they heard Him say who He was. They knew He was the Messiah. They saw Him being worshipped by others; they worshipped Him. They saw all the miracles He did, such as feeding the 5000 men, besides the women and children, and again feeding the 4000. They saw Him raise Lazarus from the dead after four days. They saw Him raise Jairus' daughter from the dead. They saw Him heal the sick, cleanse the lepers, and cast out demons from those that were oppressed of the devil. They saw Him walk on water. They saw Him die. They saw Him resurrected from the dead, and they saw Him ascend to heaven.

They believed on Him, and on and on the list goes. Having said those things, you can see that these disciples were His inner circle, and they knew Him very well. Yes, they knew Him better than the people of their day. They believed Jesus, and they laid their lives down for their belief in Him. They died for what they believed. They believed that Jesus was the Son of God. They believed that Jesus was God manifest in the flesh, and that's why many of them left their professions behind just to follow the Lord.

After He died on the cross, it looked like it was over for them. But later, they saw Him alive. They ate with Him (John 21:12) and worshipped Him. What an impact this had on these men! Even if they had not believed whatever Jesus told them in the time they spent with Him, the cross put all their doubts to an end. Jesus proved true to His word. He rose again! No man had ever risen from the dead in this form, but to make things even more interesting, He predicted His death and resurrection. This was not an average person.

Now, you can understand why they had to die for what they believed. They were willing to lay down their lives for their faith in the Lord Jesus Christ. What they believed held a higher value than their personal lives, and if their lives stood in the way of their faith, they would lay their lives down for what they believed.

After he saw Jesus resurrected and had seen his hands and touched His side, the Bible says of the disciple Thomas, "Thomas answered and said unto him, My Lord and My God" (John 20:28).

Thomas called Jesus "My Lord and MY God." He certainly knew and believed that Jesus was God, and for that reason, he was ready to lay his life down for what he believed. He went on to die for his faith in Jesus when persecuted.

Pay attention here. This man would not have laid down his life and die, believing in Jesus, if Jesus was not God. What would have been the point? I guarantee you, Thomas wouldn't have died for a lie. This man, who lived, worked, walked, and ate with Jesus, knew and strongly believed that Jesus was who He claimed to be. He saw Him crucified, die, rise again and personally met, touched and worshipped Him.

Our actions usually follow what we believe. Thomas was ready to lay down his life because he believed in Jesus. If you believe something with your whole heart, your actions will follow, otherwise it's not true faith (James 2:17-20).

Many believers, apostles, and disciples of Jesus refused to renounce their faith in Him because they knew He was truly God. Many were killed, beheaded, burned, crucified and brutalized, yet they never renounced Jesus. They would rather die believing in Jesus than to renounce Him. The sacrifice of these men's lives cannot be overlooked. It's better to die for the truth than to live for a lie. They died for the truth.

Their deaths are tremendous evidence of the truth that Jesus was who He claimed to be—God, the Savior of the World.

Some of these death references are according to tradition, while others are clearly spelled out in Scripture:

- Matthew suffered martyrdom in Ethiopia, killed by a sword wound.

- Stephen was the first martyr (Acts 7:54-60; 8:1).

- James was killed by Herod with a sword (Acts 12:2).

- John faced martyrdom when he was boiled in a huge basin of oil during a wave of persecution in Rome. However, he was miraculously delivered from death. He was then sentenced to the mines of a prison on the island of Patmos. (This is where he received and wrote the book of Revelation.)

- Bartholomew (Nathanael) was a missionary to Asia. He witnessed in present day Turkey and was martyred for his preaching in Armenia, being flayed to death by a whip.

- James, the brother of Jesus (not officially an apostle) was the leader of the church in Jerusalem. He was thrown from the southeast pinnacle of the temple when he refused to deny his faith in Jesus Christ. When they discovered that he survived the fall, his enemies beat him to death with a club.

- Thomas was stabbed with a spear in India during one of his missionary trips to establish the Church there. (Reportedly Kerala, India, in the southern part.)

- Mathias, the apostle chosen to replace Judas Iscariot, was stoned to death and beheaded.

- The apostle Paul was tortured and then beheaded by the evil emperor Nero in Rome in AD 67.

Many sources believe differently, but nevertheless, the point I'm trying to make is that all these men died for their faith in Jesus. They believed who He said He was (John 8:24), and they were willing to die for it. They wouldn't have died for a lie. They knew Jesus, and they certainly would have discovered anything untrue about Him if there was anything. There was none. Jesus was and is God. This truth is worth holding on to and dying for.

There are traditions regarding the other apostles as well but none with any reliable historical or traditional support.

Later, there were others who laid down their lives for their faith and refused to renounce Jesus. One was William Tyndale (the father of the English Bible translation), killed and martyred for his devotion to having the Bible translated into the English language so other people could learn about Jesus, who He was and what He did for us. It is believed that Tyndale was strangled and then burned at the stake.

People will die for what they believe. William Tyndale did, and so did the apostles.

My point again is that it would have been pointless for these to die for someone who wasn't God, but a mere man. For all these to lay down their lives, Jesus must be and must have been who He claimed to be—God (John 8:24).

CHAPTER SEVEN

Jesus' Statements—Who He Claimed He Was

A close examination of the Scriptures reveals that Jesus knew who He was—constantly. He again and again claimed His deity. In this chapter, we will take a look at some of His statements regarding His deity.

Jesus Did Only What He Saw the Father Do

Then answered Jesus and said unto them, Verily, verily, I say unto you, The Son can do nothing of himself, but what he seeth the Father do: for what things soever he doeth, these also doeth the Son likewise.

—John 5:19

In this verse, Jesus is stating His complete unity with the Father God (John 10:30).

We can do nothing of ourselves because we are powerless, but that was not the case with Jesus. Jesus could nothing of Himself because of **His complete unity** with the Father. It's important to understand that one part of the Godhead does not operate independent of the others. This verse further verifies the deity of Jesus. Indeed, Jesus was God. Yes, equal to God the Father.

Everything Jesus did mirrored or reflected what God the Father did. I don't know of anyone who can claim such unity in action and interdependence with God. Only Jesus could claim this because of His divine nature. There is no way Jesus could do anything the Father wasn't doing or in agreement with. He did exactly what the Father did.

My Father Is Greater than I

...for my Father is greater than I.
—John 14:28

Jesus had already claimed to be God and equal to God, which was considered by the Jews to be blasphemy at all times.

Jesus was in union with the Father, and this statement should not be viewed as a contradiction but in harmony with other scriptures.

If Jesus had already said He was God, why did He then, in this verse, have to say that the Father was greater than Him? It's important to understand that the word *greater* was only used in reference to the humanity of Jesus, not His deity. At the deity level, God the Father is not greater than God the Son; they are equal. God the Father, God the Holy Ghost, and God the Son are all equally God. None is inferior to the other.

When we look at Philippians 2:6-8 it says that Jesus did not think it was unjust to be equal with God. Why did He think that way? Because He was equal with God. Yet, He humbled Himself and became a human. Jesus was equal to God the Father in His divine nature but made Himself inferior to the Father in regard to His humanity.

When Jesus became human, He did not lose His deity, but His deity was now clothed and concealed in flesh (a human body), which has certain limitations. In this sense, the Father was greater than Jesus because He was not subject to a physical body as Jesus was. The physical part of Jesus was subject to limitations, but not His spiritual, divine nature.

Jesus and the Father Are One

I and my father are one.
—John 10:30

Jesus had already received a violent response from the people—the Jews, the scribes and the Pharisees, when He called God His Father (John 5:17-18). They understood that as Him claiming deity. Yet in this verse, He not only calls God His Father but says that He and the Father are one. The word **one** in this passage is not the regular "one" we commonly use. It means more than singleness of purpose. **It denotes a single one to the exclusion of another.** Jesus and the Father are ONE.

Note that this was the second time that Jesus claimed deity, and the Jews wanted to stone Him after His statements made in verses 29 through 38. If they had understood His statements to mean that He wasn't proclaiming His deity, then they would have left Him alone.

A Witness of Myself and the Witness of the Father

I am the one that bear witness of myself, and the Father that sent me beareth witness of me.
—John 8:18

Here, Jesus makes a distinction between Himself and the Father and uses Himself and the Father as two different witnesses to fulfill the requirement of Deuteronomy 17:6. Jesus would have been deceiving these Jews if there was no distinction between His Father and Himself; and yet, they are ONE (John 10:30; 1 John 5:7). This is a great mystery, yet a very well established fact laid out in scripture.

Note: Jesus did many miracles, but they were not done from the power of His deity. They were done in His humanity by the Holy Spirit (Acts 10:38) and putting faith in the Father, just as we must all do. This makes it easier to relate to and understand John 14:12.

Ye Shall Die in Your Sins... I Am He

I said therefore unto you, that ye shall die in your sins: for if ye believe not that I am he, ye shall die in your sins.

—John 8:24

Here Jesus proclaims Himself as "I am." In Exodus 3:14 when God revealed Himself to Moses, He proclaimed and identified Himself as "I am."

God the Father calls Himself *I am* (Ex. 3:14), and Jesus calls Himself *I am* three times (John 8:24, 8:28, 8:58). Jesus was the great *I am* of Exodus 3:14, manifest in the flesh (1 Tim. 3:16).

Also, right before His crucifixion in the garden of Gethsemane, Jesus said, "I am," and just that statement knocked the 600 men who came to arrest Him backwards to the ground. There was tremendous power in the words *I am*, just as when it was spoken to Moses (Ex. 3:14).

Another important part of John 8:24 is that it says, "If ye believe not that I am he, ye shall die in your sins."

This verse is saying that failure to believe and acknowledge that Jesus is the "I AM" (God) (Ex. 3:14), then you can't be saved and shall die in your sins. Why? Because Jesus was God, and if He wasn't, then you will die in your sins, and all mankind is doomed. Hallelujah! Since He was God, there is hope for mankind. Man can be saved through faith in Jesus Christ.

If we do not believe that Jesus was God, then we can't be saved. Jesus in His humanity alone could not save the world. It would be impossible because He had to be God. If we believe in a "Jesus" lesser than God, we can't truly be saved. Jesus = God. We can't have a relationship with God without receiving Jesus. Jesus was God, and that invites us into a relationship with God the Father. Jesus was and is God with us—Emmanuel.

Convinceth Me of Sin?

Which of you convinceth me of sin? And if I say the truth, why do ye not believe me?
—John 8:46

Raise your hand if you would make such a statement. If you raised your hand, you are a hypocrite! You are a liar. No one can stand and say they have no sin. The only exception was and is Jesus.

No one among this mob would find any sin in Jesus' life. If they would have had any indictment against Jesus, they certainly would have spoken up in response to Jesus' question.

But God's Word says that "all have sinned and come short of

the glory of God" (Rom. 3:23). The "all" this verse speaks about is *all men*, but even though Jesus was a man, this verse does not include Him because He never sinned—thus this question, "Which of you convinceth me of sin?"

A comparison of these two scriptures reveals that Jesus did not sin. God cannot sin. Because Jesus was God in the flesh (1 Tim. 3:16), He never sinned (2 Cor. 5:21; Heb. 4:15, 7:26). 1 Peter 2:22 says that Jesus did not sin. Although Pilate was not a godly man, he willfully said he had found no fault in this man, Jesus (Luke 23:4, 14-22; Matt. 27:19).

Before Abraham Was, I Am

Jesus said unto them, Verily, verily, I say unto you, Before Abraham was, I am.

—John 8:58

Here, Jesus goes on to say that He existed before Abraham and again associated Himself with the great "I am" statement of Exodus 3:14: "And God said unto Moses, I AM THAT I AM; and he said, thus shalt thou say unto the children of Israel, I AM hath sent me unto you." This statement could leave no doubt that Jesus was claiming deity in the highest sense of the word.

Jesus was God. Since Jesus was the one who created Abraham, He existed before him, and this was an accurate statement.

I Am the Way, the Truth and the Life

Jesus saith unto him, I am the way, the truth, and the life: no man cometh unto the Father, but by me.

—John 14:6

Jesus did not say He was **a** way, **a** truth and **a** life. No! He claimed to be **the Way, the Truth** and **the Life**.

This leaves no room for other means of salvation. This statement leaves no alternatives. Any religion that doesn't acknowledge Jesus as the ONLY way of salvation is in error and false.

The word **the** is a definite article. Jesus is not just the way... FULL STOP. He is also the truth and the life. If Jesus is not the LORD of your life, you have missed the truth. Jesus = Truth.

Notice also that it says "NO man comes to the Father except through Jesus." If Jesus is not the Lord of your life, you have missed God. I don't care if you say you "believe in God." If you reject Jesus, you have rejected the True Life. Jesus = Life. No Jesus, no life. No Jesus, no Father.

The Lord Our God Is One Lord

And Jesus answered him, The first of all the commandments is, Hear, O Israel; The Lord our God is one Lord.
—Mark 12:29

In this verse, Jesus quoted Deuteronomy 6:4, "...The Lord our God is one Lord." It's important to understand that there are not two or three Gods, yet Jesus claimed to be God just like God the Father. This union is a mystery, which the church has come to call "the Trinity" (Father, Son, and Holy Spirit), all one Lord. It might look like it defies human understanding, but it does not defy spiritual understanding. I have learned that there are two types of understanding: natural and spiritual (Col. 1:9).

If something doesn't make sense in the natural (to your mind), it can still be accepted and believed because it makes sense according to spiritual understanding (in your spirit). For instance, healing: Someone can be prayed for and healed without seeing a doctor or taking a pill. People have been healed of all sorts of "incurable diseases" like cancer, AIDS, etc. How is that possible according to your natural, human understanding? Yet it has happened, and it still does.

Well, it is because there is a spiritual realm or world that calls for spiritual understanding and spiritual logic. It is actually a more real world than the physical world. That relates to the truth that Jesus is Lord. He is God. "The Lord our God is one Lord" (Deut. 6:4).

Believe the Works

But if I do, though ye believe not me, believe the works: that ye may know, and believe, that the Father is in me, and I in him.

—John 10:38

Miracles are great witnesses to the power of God, and here, Jesus tells the Jews to at least believe the miracles, signs, and wonders He did. Then they would know that He is God (one with the Father) and that Father is in Him, and He is in the Father. He was saying that considering the signs and wonders would open their hearts to believe in who He had said He was, "I and the Father are one" (John 10:30).

The Father is in Jesus, and Jesus is in Him. This is expressing a great degree of unity. I can't even find the right words to explain it. John 10:30 sums it up.

Ye Say Well

*Ye call me Master and Lord: and ye say well;
for so I am. If I then, your Lord and Master, have
washed your feet; ye also ought to wash one another's feet.*

—John 13:13-14

In this passage of scripture, Jesus said that His disciples called Him *Lord*. He went on to say that they said the right thing to call Him Lord because He was. Deuteronomy 6:4 says, "The Lord our God is one Lord." Jesus is Lord. Jesus was and still is God.

Think about this for a moment. If Jesus was not LORD, He would not have commended the disciples for calling Him *LORD*. He would have rebuked them.

Chapter Eight

Honoring the Son = Honoring the Father

That all men should honour the Son, even as they honour the Father. He that honoureth not the Son honoureth not the Father which hath sent him.
—John 5:23

This is one of the strongest arguments of a well-established truth in Scripture: Jesus was and truly is God. We can't just honor Jesus, but we have to honor Him *even as* (in like manner or the same way) we honor the Father. If you do not honor Jesus, you have not honored the Father. There is no way around this. You can't dishonor the LORD in an effort to honor the Father. As a matter of fact, you can't even know the Father without Jesus because Jesus reveals the Father to us all.

This is what draws a line and separates true Christianity from the religions of the world. Most religions honor Jesus as a great man (examples: Jehovah's Witnesses, Islam, and the Unification Church, etc.) but are violently opposed to making Jesus equal to the Almighty God (1 John 2:23).

This scripture also says *all* men, not just a few but *all*. If you are a human being, this scripture applies to you. It's speaking to you.

Knowing Jesus = Knowing the Father

Then said they unto him, Where is thy Father? Jesus answered, Ye neither know me, nor my Father:

*if ye had known me, ye should have known my
Father also.*

—John 8:19

Here, we see Jesus calling God *His Father*. John 5:18 verifies that Jesus was equal to God the Father. That's why He called Him "my father."

Jesus also said that if they had known Him, they would have known the Father as well. Knowing Jesus is knowing the Father. This establishes that Jesus was God and that Jesus and the Father are ONE, just as John 10:30 says. This is saying that a person who doesn't know (have personal relationship with) Jesus, doesn't know the Father.

Anyone who says that you can have a relationship with God the Father without first believing on God the Son, Jesus Christ, such as Jehovah's Witnesses, the Unification Church, Mormons, Jesuits, the Unity Church, Islam and many others, is teaching error and has the spirit of anti-Christ. (1 John 4:3; 2 John 7-9).

Jesus is **the** way to the Father, not "*a way.*" There is no short cut. If you don't believe and receive Jesus as your Lord and Savior, you cannot claim to have or know the Father. If you let Jesus in, the Father comes in along with Him, but you can't let the Father in without letting in Jesus first.

*If ye had known me, ye should have known my
Father also: and from henceforth ye know him,
and have seen him.*

—John 14:7

This verse also clearly shows that knowing Jesus is knowing the Father. This is not only because Jesus did what He saw the Father do, but because He was God in the flesh—God with us. Knowing Jesus equates to knowing the Father because they are **one**, but you can't know the Father without knowing Jesus first. In other words, relationship starts with Jesus before it goes to the Father. Anyone who tries bypassing Jesus is joking. If you know Jesus, you will know the Father. Until you are in a relationship with Jesus, you can't have a relationship with God the Father. Jesus is the door to relationship with the Father.

Again, Knowing Jesus = Knowing the Father. However, knowing the Father does not equal knowing Jesus because you can't know the Father unless you first know Jesus.

Receiving Jesus = Receiving the Father

...he that receiveth me receiveth him that sent me.
—John 13:20

This is another powerful passage in line with all my other statements. Here, Jesus continues to emphasize that receiving Him is receiving God the Father who sent Him. Jesus was equal to the Father (John 10:30). Receiving Him is equivalent to receiving the Father because they are one (John 10:30, 14:6-7).

Denying Jesus is denying God. Acknowledging Jesus is acknowledging God (1 John 2:23). Hating Jesus is hating God (John 15:23). Honoring Jesus is honoring God (John 5:23) because Jesus is God and is equal to God the Father.

Hating Jesus = Hating the Father

He that hateth me hateth my Father also.
—John 15:23

Oh boy, this is a powerful verse! How many religions or people hate Jesus, yet claim to be in relationship with God? This is one more verse in a list of scriptures in which Jesus equated any form of rejection of Him or who He claimed as rejection of God the Father.

Say it like this: Rejecting or Hating Jesus = Rejecting or Hating the Father. Any group or religion that claims to have access to God the Father without exalting Jesus to an equal position is completely deceived. Hating Jesus is hating God because Jesus is God and equal to the Father (John 10:30; Phil. 2:6).

Chapter nine

The Sinlessness of Jesus

The sinlessness of Jesus is a vital doctrine in Scripture. It is foundational to Christianity because if Jesus had been a sinner Himself, then He too would have needed a savior. He certainly couldn't have been anyone else's savior. But Jesus was so pure that even His enemies attested to His innocence and purity.

Jesus was the only man that never had any sin in His life. He never sinned (2 Cor. 5:21; 1 Peter 2:22). Jesus was able to pay for our sins because He was God and the sinless sacrificial Lamb. He had no sins of His own to pay for. Hallelujah!

> *Which of you convinceth me of sin? And if I say the truth, why do ye not believe me?*
> —John 8:46

No man can stand and say he has no sin. The Bible says that "all have sinned and come short of the glory of God" (Rom. 3:23). Jesus was the only exception to this truth because He was not just a man. He was more than a man. He was God—Man. He was God in a physical body. That's why He asked these Jews a question they could not answer. Jesus had no sin in His life that these people could point out. If Jesus had committed even one single sin, this mob would have spoken up. He had none, and these Jews knew it.

> *Who did no sin, neither was guile found in his mouth.*
>
> —1 Peter 2:22

Here is yet another scripture attesting to the fact that Jesus never sinned. What a testimony of His divinity. He never spoke in deceit. He committed no sin. How much clearer can that get?

This is a vital issue. If Jesus was a sinner, then His life was not holy enough to atone for the whole human race. But if He was the sinless Son of God, then His life was worth more than **all** of humanity. This also testifies of His deity. Surely, Jesus was God.

> *And he made his grave with the wicked, and with the rich in his death; because he had done no violence, neither was any deceit in his mouth.*
>
> —Isaiah 53:9

This prophecy was about Jesus. Years before Jesus came on the scene, the prophet Isaiah prophesied, and evidently the Scriptures show that Jesus did no violence and spoke no deceit. In other words, He never committed sin.

> *For we have not a high priest which cannot be touched with the feeling of our infirmities; but was in all points tempted like as were, yet without sin.*
>
> —Hebrews 4:15

This verse clearly states that although Jesus became like one of us and was tempted (Matt. 4:1-4) like all of us, He was still without sin.

For such an high priest became us, who is holy, harmless, undefiled, separate from sinners, and made higher than the heavens.

—Hebrews 7:26

All of these qualities of Jesus were mentioned in comparison to the Old Testament priests. They had to be holy, harmless, undefiled, and separate from sinners. Jesus was all of these things in a way that no sinful man could ever be. Plus, He was not only exalted in the eyes of men as the high priest was, but He was exalted to sit at the right hand of God—as God. Jesus was better in every way.

What a paradox and a necessity that we, who were unholy, harmful, defiled, and companions of sinners, would have Jesus be our High Priest, ever living to intercede for us.

No one has ever been able to point out a single sin Jesus committed because He never committed any. He broke some of the Jewish traditions and interpretations of the Law, like the Sabbath, but He wasn't in error. Their interpretations were in error.

CHAPTER TEN

Four Facts of Jesus' Deity

Fact 1: Worship

One of the most unique and special things that is reserved for God alone is worship.

Although many men desire worship and try to elevate themselves to be worshipped, the truth remains that only God alone is worthy of worship (Isa. 42:8).

Thousands of scriptures refer to men worshiping God. The lesser (man) worships the greater (God). We see the scriptures commanding people to worship the Lord, and they did—David, Saul, Jehoshaphat, Samuel, etc.

In Daniel 3, we see three Hebrew men that refused to worship the golden image that King Nebuchadnezzar had set up. These men (Shadrach, Meshach, and Abednego) knew very well that God alone was and is worthy of worship, and they refused to bow down and worship the image, even when they knew the consequences of their refusal was death in a fiery furnace.

What a terrific attitude these men had! It's definitely worth a mention. They were true believers and refused to bend, bow, budge or burn. They were thrown into a fiery furnace, heated seven times hotter than it was normally heated, but the three Hebrew men would not burn. They came out of the fiery furnace after the king realized they couldn't burn and saw an angel as the fourth person in the fire (Dan. 3:25).

What a miracle for not bowing and worshiping anything but God Almighty. God supernaturally delivered the three Hebrew men, and when they came out, they didn't even smell like smoke, neither were their clothes burned. Now that's a miracle!

Daniel 3 gives the entire account of these three men. But one other amazing thing is that after the king realized that Shadrach, Meshach, and Abednego were worshiping the only true, living God, he commanded that no one should dare say a thing against the God of Shadrach, Meshach, and Abednego, otherwise, they would be cut into pieces, and their houses made a dung hill because "there is no other God that can deliver after this sort" (Dan. 3:29).

Now all that being said, here is my point: Only God deserves worship—nothing nor anyone else. These three men laid down their lives because they believed such. Their lives were so irrelevant to them that they wouldn't let them be a barrier to what they believed. They would rather lay their lives down than to compromise their belief that only God was worthy of worship, not Nebuchadnezzar.

These Jews would not worship any other man because they knew only God is worthy of worship. Yet many Jews and others worshipped Jesus many times during His lifetime. Why? It's because He was and is God. He deserved the worship. They knew and believed that Jesus was God—God manifest in the flesh (physical body).

Here are eleven instances where Jesus was worshipped. Eight of them are mentioned by Matthew, Mark, Luke and John. (Matt. 2:2; 2:11; 8:2; 9:18; 14:33; 15:25; 20:20; 28:9, 17; Mark 5:6; Luke 24:52; John 9:38). The fact that Jesus received the worship of these people further attests to the fact that He was God manifest in the flesh (1 Tim. 3:16). He was and is God.

a) Wise men - "...and fell down and worshipped Him..." (Matt. 2:11).

In this scripture, we see the wise men worship Jesus at His birth. They travelled purposely to worship Him. It's important to understand that Jesus did not grow into becoming God. He was God even at His birth. As a young child or a baby, Jesus was God in a physical body.

The Bible says they fell down and worshipped Jesus. Now, why did these men travel thousands of miles to worship a little child? What did they know or believe about Jesus? They knew that Jesus was more than a man or a little child. They knew He was God, so they travelled to worship Him. They were pretty smart, right? Right! They deserve credit for worshiping God.

Notice that in Matthew 2:7, they didn't fall down and worship Herod when they were called in by him. They knew he wasn't God and wasn't worthy of even a little bit of worship. They reserved their worship for Jesus, whom they knew and believed was God and worthy of all worship. It didn't matter if He was still a child; He was God anyway. These men were indeed wise men. Also, I would like to add that these wise men were not Jews, yet they knew that Jesus was not just the King of the Jews, but King of all.

Jesus was God, and deserved worship, even at His birth, which He received (Matt. 2:11). No wonder these men were wise men. *Surely* wise men!

b) A leper - "...There came a leper and worshipped him..." (Matt. 8:2).

Here we see a leper coming to Jesus and worshiping Him. Why did this leper choose to worship Jesus? There were many sorcerers and many rulers and men in authority in his time. Why did this leper, of all men, choose to worship Jesus? It's seems obvious that this man knew something about Jesus or got a revelation that encouraged him to worship Jesus. This man also knew that worship was for God alone. This leper knew that Jesus must be God, the Savior of the world. He worshipped Jesus because He was God and deserved his worship. And you know what? He was rewarded for it. Jesus healed him (Matt. 8:3). I don't believe this leper went about worshiping whomever he met, even if it was out of desperation to be healed. He knew who deserved to be worshipped, and he did so as soon as he saw Jesus.

Worship is reserved for God alone (Matt. 4:10).

Angels refused worship (Rev. 19:10; 22:8-9), and men refused worship (Acts 10:25-26; 14:11-18). The fact that Jesus received this man's worship further attests to the fact that He was God in the flesh (1 Tim. 3:16). So the leper, in my opinion, had a revelation of who Jesus was, and that played a part in his healing.

c) Jairus - "While he spake these things unto them, behold, there came a certain ruler, and worshipped him, saying, My daughter is even now dead: but come and lay thy hand upon her, and she shall live" (Matt. 9:18).

This verse says this man was a ruler. He was a man in authority. Yet, he came and worshipped Jesus. Usually rulers are the kind of people who would want to be worshipped. They are looked upon as greater. But this ruler humbled himself and realized that worship is reserved for God alone, and when he came to Jesus, he rightfully gave Him the worship He deserved.

Jesus was and is God and deserves all the honor, glory and worship (John 5:23).

A ruler worshipped Jesus. I believe he knew what he was doing, and it was not a shameful thing to do. It's not shameful to worship God. Men in higher authority, leaders and rulers must worship God, and we see a good example from this ruler in the above passage.

d) The disciples - "Then they that were in the ship came and worshipped him…" (Matt. 14:33).

The disciples lived walked, ate and did almost everything with Jesus. They knew Jesus better than any other man during their time. And many times, we see them worshiping Jesus. Here, after the wind ceased, they had seen Jesus walk on water, and save Peter from drowning, as soon as He got in the boat, they **worshipped Him**.

The disciples worshipped God. They worshipped Jesus. Surely, like the wise men, the leper and the ruler, they knew and believed that Jesus was the Son of God and deserved worship, so they did worship Him—again and again.

Jesus deserves all the worship because He is God.

e) The disciples again - "……and they worshipped him" (Matt. 28:17; Luke 24:52).

Jesus had already risen and appeared to the disciples. At this point, He was ascending to heaven, and the same disciples that worshipped Him in the boat after He calmed the storm worshipped Him again. Surely, Jesus was God, otherwise the disciples wouldn't have worshipped Him.

f) Yet again, the disciples - "… And they came and held Him by the feet and worshipped Him" (Matt. 28:9).

The disciples worshipped Jesus once more right after His resurrection. This is another time among many that His disciples worshipped Him. If Jesus wasn't really God, the disciples wouldn't have still been worshiping Him. They would have known it if Jesus wasn't who He claimed to be.

Jesus was worshipped from birth until He ascended back to heaven. This speaks volumes of who Jesus was. Jesus could not have been a mere man.

g) A demon-possessed man – "But when he saw Jesus afar off, he ran and worshipped him, And cried with a loud voice, and said, What have I to do with thee, Jesus, *thou* Son of the most high God? I adjure thee by God, that thou torment me not" (Mark 5:6).

Here we see a man who was demon possessed running and worshiping Jesus. Of his own free will, he chose to worship Jesus. Why did this man choose to worship Jesus of all men? It seems as though he knew who Jesus was. This demon-possessed man "cried out with a loud voice and said…Jesus, thou Son of the Most High God." This man called Jesus the Son of God, which literally means "God in the flesh" and that Jesus is equal to God.

So this man did not just worship anyone at any time. Although he was demon possessed, Satan cannot control people completely without their consent. This man believed Jesus was the Lord God, and this truth worked to this man's benefit because Jesus went on to cast out the "unclean spirit."

h) Blind, healed man – "...Jesus heard that they had cast him out; and when he had found him, he said unto him, Dost thou believe on the Son of God? He answered and said, Who is he, Lord, that I might believe on him? And Jesus said unto him, Thou hast both seen him, and it is he that talketh with thee. And he said, Lord, I believe. And he worshipped him" (John 9:35-38).

Here in this passage of scripture is another man who did not know that Jesus was the Son of God, yet when Jesus told him who He was, the blind, healed man confessed, "Lord I believe. And he worshipped Him."

This man confessed and, through his actions, went on to worship Jesus. He worshipped God. Again, this man must have known or gotten a revelation of who Jesus was. Jesus is the Lord God and deserves all the worship, and we can learn from this blind, healed man as well.

i) A Canaanite woman - (Matt. 15:22-25).

j) The mother of Zebedee's children - (Matt. 20:20).

k) Lydia - (Acts 16:14).

This scripture tells of a woman named Lydia who worshipped God. She did not worship man, but God.

Since Jesus was worshipped and accepted the worship, we can know without a doubt that He was God. And just as we learned earlier that worship is reserved for God alone, we can see that Lydia did the right thing by worshiping God. Jesus was and is God. Jesus = God. Worshiping Jesus is worshiping God because Jesus is God.

l) Justus worshipped God (Acts 18:7).

A Lesson from the Apostle Peter

And as Peter was coming in, Cornelius met him, and fell down at his feet, and worshipped him. But Peter took him up, saying, Stand up; I myself also am a man.

—Acts 10:25-26

This passage of scripture is very informative. Cornelius was a devout man who feared God, and it just so happened that he was instructed by the angel to call for Peter the Apostle who would tell him about the Lord. As soon as Peter came into Cornelius' house, he fell down at Peter's feet and worshipped him. But look at Peter's response. He **immediately** took him up, saying, "Stand up; I am a man—not God." Peter was saying I am not God, so don't waste time worshiping me, get up quickly.

Let me ask, what did Peter believe or know? Why did he refuse worship? Peter knew that he was not God, and he knew that worship was for God alone. Peter never took the worship that was offered to him by Cornelius. He immediately rejected it, saying, "I myself also am a man." Peter knew that a man was not worthy of worship. Worship is God's alone, not for man (Isa. 42:8).

.

Peter not only rejected worship, but in so doing, he rejected any claim to deity. Had he accepted worship, it would have been blasphemy on his part for claiming to be God. Peter made his share of blunders but not this time. Many times, when Peter opened his mouth, it was to change feet, but give him credit. This time he hit the nail right on the head. Peter refused the worship that belonged to God alone.

There is not a single instance when Jesus told those that worshipped Him, "Stand up; I myself am also a man." He gladly accepted worship because He was God. Never did He reject worship, unlike Peter.

Here in this instance we see Cornelius worshiping Peter. However, we see Peter worshiping Jesus, which meant He knew that Jesus was God (Matt. 14:33; Luke 24:52). Peter, the lesser, worshipped Jesus, the greater.

A Lesson from the Apostle Paul

In Acts 14:8-16, Paul healed a man that was a cripple from his mother's womb and had never walked. When the people saw this miracle, they decided that they were going to burn incense and sacrifice in worship of Paul and Barnabas. But when Paul and Barnabas heard this, they tore their clothes as a sign of showing unworthiness and told the people, "We are men of like passions with you...." Paul and Barnabas were saying that there was nothing special about them because they were "men" just like them and did not deserve or accept any form of worship. In other words, they weren't God to accept and receive worship.

Why didn't Paul and Barnabas just accept and enjoy the worship? Why did they have to refuse the worship and sacrifice? Well, the answer is simple. They weren't God. Paul and Barnabas knew that worship was reserved for God alone, and accepting worship would be blasphemy and exalting themselves to God's level. So they had to reject any form of worship.

Now why didn't Jesus refuse worship all the times He was worshipped and called the Son of God, Lord, God or Lord God?

Look, it would have been blasphemy for Jesus to receive worship if He was not God. Jesus accepted and received worship because He was God and is God. Jesus was God, and if He had acted like Paul and Barnabas, refusing worship, then He would have been denying that He was God, which would have reduced Him to a mere man, making His death useless for the world. Hallelujah, He never rejected worship!

He never said, "Hey guys, don't worship me. I am just a man; I am not God." He never said He was unworthy the way Peter, Paul and Barnabas did. No, Jesus always accepted and received worship all the way. It doesn't surprise me because before He became a man, He was worshipped daily by the angels in heaven.

So Jesus receiving worship further proves and endorses that He was God and indeed worthy to be worshipped.

Fact 2: Forgiveness of Sins

Just like worship, forgiveness of sins is an attribute reserved for God alone.

> *When Jesus saw their faith, he said unto the sick of the palsy, Son, thy sins be forgiven thee. But there were certain of the scribes sitting there, and*

> *reasoning in their hearts, why doth this man speak*
> *blasphemies? Who can forgive sins but God only?*
> —Mark 2:5-7

Jesus told the sick of palsy, "Son, thy sins be forgiven thee." But the scribes asked, "Who can forgive sins but God only?"

I am asking you the same question. Who has the power to forgive sins? Who can forgive sins?

A simple and clear answer would be that God alone has the power and authority to forgive sins. Now, since that is true, then Jesus has to be God in order to forgive sins, right? Right, Jesus was God, and He knew that He had the power to forgive sins. That's why He did so for this man and on other occasions.

Also, the scribes that heard Jesus say, "Thy sins be forgiven thee," understood that only God had the power and authority to do so. That's why they said, "Why doth this man speak blasphemies?" They called Jesus' statements blasphemy—mainly because they never knew who He was. Had they had known, they would have never said that. It was ignorance of who Jesus was on their part because Jesus plainly and publically declared who He was and the Scriptures told about Him. Yet these "elite" scribes just didn't get it (Mk. 2:7).

Luke 11:4 is the part of the Lord's Prayer that teaches us to ask God for forgiveness, right? Right. Why do we have to ask God to forgive our sins? It's only because God alone has the power to forgive sins.

If we confess our sins, he is faithful and just to forgive
us our sins, and to cleanse us from all unrighteousness.
—1 John 1:9

God is faithful and just to forgive our sins. God is the **only** one who can forgive our sins and cleanse us from all unrighteousness. Jesus forgave sins and still does. Why Jesus? Because He is God, He has the power and right to do so.

Priests do not have the power to forgive sins. They themselves have their own sins. It would be logical to think that for someone to forgive sins, he himself ought to be sinless—without sin. Well, as we covered earlier, Jesus was sinless. He was God, and so He forgave sins and still forgives sins.

Wherefore I say unto thee, Her sins, which are
many, are forgiven; for she loved much: but to
whom little is forgiven, the same loveth little. And
he said unto her, Thy sins are forgiven.
—Luke 7:47-48

We saw in Mark 2:5-7 an account of a man with palsy whom Jesus healed and forgave his sins, but the scribes, reasoning in their hearts, were like, *why does this man speak blasphemies?* "Who can forgive sins but God only?" they asked.

This question was raised in the hearts of the scribes as a result of Jesus saying, "Thy sins be forgiven thee," so we can assume as well that a similar question would have been raised here at Luke 7:47-48 by the same scribes had they been present.

This is the second time that Jesus forgave people's sins. Jesus forgave the sins of this woman (Luke 7:48), just as He did the man with palsy (Mark 2:1-7). Why? Jesus was God, and He had the power, the right and the authority to forgive sins. If He was another ordinary man, He would have no right or power to forgive sins, which would be blasphemy. For who can forgive sins but God only? (Mark 2:1-7)

So in conclusion, Jesus was and is God. He had the right, power and authority to forgive sins, and that's why He did so. His deity gave Him the ability and the right to forgive sins. Only God can forgive the sins of mankind. Jesus forgave and died for these sins—for He was God.

Fact 3: Creation

Just like worship and forgiving sins, this is another attribute reserved for God alone.

> Hast thou not known? hast thou not heard that the everlasting God, the LORD, the Creator of the ends of the earth, fainteth not, neither is weary? there is no searching of his understanding.
> —Isaiah 40:28

> For unto us a child is born, unto us a son is given: and the government shall be upon his shoulder: and his name shall be called Wonderful, Counseller, The mighty God, The everlasting Father, the prince of peace.
> —Isaiah 9:6

Looking at both of these scriptures, Isaiah 40:28 says that the everlasting God is the Lord, the Creator of the ends of the earth.

So it's very clear that God is the Creator. But then Isaiah 9:6 calls Jesus the everlasting Father, the mighty God. Since God is the Creator, and Jesus is God, then Jesus is the Creator.

The term everlasting God and everlasting Father are used interchangeably, so Everlasting Father = Everlasting God.

> *All things were made by him; and without him*
> *was not anything made that was made. In him was*
> *life; and the life was the light of men.*
> —John 1:3

Jesus is the subject of this scripture. Jesus is the Creator of all things—heaven, earth, human beings, etc. Nothing existed on its own. Order did not come out of chaos as evolution teaches. We are created beings, created by God—Jesus. Jesus is the architect of the human body with all its complexity. It's insanity to believe that chaos would produce the order that is as complex as a human body with all its tissues, veins, organisms, fibers, blood cells, DNA, blood types, enzymes, arteries, etc. What is the probability of dropping a bomb in a jet factory and getting a well assembled jet ready to fly? I leave that to you to figure out! Let me go on to say that it takes more faith to believe in evolution than to believe in creation. There is no evidence for this phony science! How can order come out of chaos? How can nothing make something?

Evolution is an astounding joke, and it's is not science. As a matter of fact, it's a religion—a manmade religion or belief system of the immoral and ungodly. It's completely flawed. Most people who promote that kind of ideology also live a totally ungodly lifestyle. It's a scapegoat for them. Because they believe there is no Creator, they can indulge themselves in immoral lifestyles without restraint and give no account for their behavior. They believe they are accountable to no one since to them God does not exist (Psa. 14:1; 53:1). For these kinds of people, there are no moral absolutes. To them, all things are permissible.

I believe one of the reasons evolution is now embedded in our school systems' curriculum is because these people want to indoctrinate our children at an early age. I also believe they do so to get federal funding by masquerading this religion as science. I promise you that if evolution were to be called by its true name—a religion—government funding would disappear.

It's important to understand that Jesus created you in His own image. Jesus created all things, and nothing existed that wasn't created by Him.

> *For by him were all things created, that are in heaven, and that are in earth, visible and invisible, whether they be thrones, or dominions, or principalities, or powers: all things were created by him, and for him: And he is before all things, and by him all things consist.* —Colossians 1:16-17

Here, another scripture continues to confirm and endorse Jesus as Creator, confirming that He is God, since God is the Creator (Isa. 40:28). The heaven and the earth and the things therein were all created by Jesus. Those we can see, and those we can't. They were all created by Him for Himself (Isa. 43:7).

We were created for and belong to God. Jesus not only created all things, period, but He also holds them together. They all exist through Him.

It's undeniable that Jesus is God with all these terrific facts and truths. Since the creator is God, and Jesus is the Creator, then Jesus is God.

Fact 4: Savior

Just like worship, forgiving of sins, and creation, this is another attribute reserved for God alone.

A close study of Scriptures clearly reveals that Jesus is the Savior of mankind. Many times you will find Jesus being referred to as the Savior.

> *And my spirit hath rejoiced in God my savior.*
> —Luke 1:47

God is called the Savior. Mary rejoiced in God, her Savior. Of whom was she speaking? She was speaking of Jesus, her Savior and God.

She said God was her Savior. So we can clearly see that God is our Savior, based on Mary's statement in Luke 1:47.

> *For unto you is born this day in the city of David a*
> *Saviour, which is Christ the Lord.*
> —Luke 2:11

The angel appeared to shepherds and announced the birth of Jesus. But notice that the angel called Jesus "Saviour, which is Christ the Lord."

Mary, the mother of Jesus, called God *her Savior*, the angel called Jesus *Savior*. This clarifies that Jesus is the God that Mary called her Savior. So Jesus is God, the Savior.

The word *Lord* is used interchangeably with *God*, which means they are the same.

Now, let me ask a question. Can a mere man be the Savior of the whole world? If Jesus was only a man, and not God, what would make Him the Savior? There is no way another man could be the Savior of the world. If someone is to be the Savior, He has to be God, not only a man. Mary and the angels understood this, and so should you and I.

That's why I continue to show you that Jesus was God.

Most will agree that God is the only Savior, but some do not believe that Jesus was and is God. Why would someone put faith in Jesus as his or her Savior if they never believed He was God? To believe in Jesus as your Savior, you must firmly believe He is who He said He was and what Scripture repeatedly teaches about Him—that He is God in the flesh. If you don't, then how can He be your Savior? (John 8:24) Can just an angel, as some believe, be your savior or can someone inferior to God be your savior and the savior of the entire world? It's got to be more than a mere man or else anyone could be the savior of the whole world.

See, God could not find a man good enough or completely perfect to save the whole human race. That's why He had to do it Himself by becoming a physical human (Jesus). God became man and became the Savior of the whole world (John 4:42). Jesus was God in a physical body.

I think it is important to think about this. It's that pivotal. It's also amazing to see that Mary rejoiced in God, her Savior. She fully understood that God was her Savior. She was rejoicing in

Jesus as her Savior because later, when Jesus grew up, He went on to be her Savior on the cross.

Additionally, the angel sent by God to the shepherds would have been ignorant to call Jesus *Savior* if He truly wasn't. Actually the angel's message was not his message, but God's. God instructed this angel to say so. So it was God the Father who really called Jesus "Christ the LORD," the Savior of the world. The angel called Him Savior because He was truly the Savior.

If I were to write this mathematically, it would be: God = Savior = Jesus or Jesus = Savior = God. This clearly illustrates what Mary and the angel said in Luke 1:47 and Luke 2:11.

Philippians 3:20 says that the Lord Jesus Christ is **the** Savior. 1 Timothy 1:1 calls Jesus, "God our Saviour." 1 Timothy 2:3 says that God is our Savior. 1 Timothy 4:10 says the Living God is the Savior of all men.

Honestly speaking, you cannot just ignore all these scriptures that call Jesus Savior, God and Living God. These scriptures clearly endorse the truth that Jesus is God. Yes, God the Savior of all men (1 Tim. 4:10).

These are striking truths that shouldn't be ignored or overlooked.

> But hath in due times manifested his word through preaching, which is committed unto me according to the commandment of <u>God our Saviour</u>, To Titus, mine own son after the common faith: Grace, mercy, and peace, from God the Father and <u>the Lord Jesus Christ our Saviour.</u>
> —Titus 1:3-4 (underline mine)

Here as well, we see another scripture calling God our Savior, and it follows up to say that Jesus is our Savior. This then means that God our Savior is Jesus Christ or Jesus Christ our Savior is God our Savior. It illustrates clearly that Jesus is God.

> ...the great God and our Saviour Jesus Christ.
> —Titus 2:13

Jesus our Savior is the great God this verse is talking about. Jesus was truly and is truly the great God.

Other Scriptures

> And without controversy great is the mystery of godliness: God was manifest in the flesh, justified in the Spirit, seen of angels, preached unto the Gentiles, believed on in the world, received up into glory.
> —1 Timothy 3:16 (underline mine)

This scripture is another of many outstanding ones that clearly endorse the deity of Jesus.

When was God manifested in the flesh or received up in glory? Of course this happened only in the life and ministry of Jesus. Therefore, this is a very clear reference to Jesus being God.

Jesus was God manifest in the flesh (John 1:1, 14). The words "in the flesh" refer to the incarnation of Jesus Christ into a physical body, and are a direct reference to the deity of Jesus.

Jesus was justified in the Spirit. Jesus was sinless (John 8:46; 1 Pet. 2:22; Heb.7:26; 2 Cor. 5:21).

He was seen of angels. Jesus was constantly observed by the angels at His birth, during his temptation, at the tomb, and at His ascension.

He was preached unto the Gentiles. He was preached to the nations. God ordained that the gospel of Christ is for all nations (Matt. 24:14).

Jesus was believed on in the world. Everywhere Jesus is preached, faith comes (Rom.10:17), and new believers are added to the body of Christ.

Jesus was received up into glory. This is referring to His ascension back to heaven after His resurrection (Acts 1:9-11).

So we can clearly see that Jesus is the person that 1 Timothy 3:16 is describing as God manifest in the flesh.

> *All things that the Father hath are mine: therefore said I, that he shall take of mine, and shall shew it unto you.*
> —John 16:15

Jesus clearly said that **ALL** things that the Father hath are His. All means all—everything. John 10:30 says that Jesus and the Father are equal. They are one. Jesus is saying that what belongs to the Father belongs to Him because He is **ONE** with the Father.

That's why receiving Jesus and receiving God are the same thing because everything that is true of the Father is true of Jesus. You cannot receive God without receiving Jesus first. It won't work like that (John 14:6-9; 5:23; 8:19).

*What and if ye shall see the Son of man ascend up
where he was before?*

—John 6:62

If these people had a hard time believing Jesus came down from heaven, what would they do when they saw Him ascend into heaven? This talk was rare as hen's teeth. Jesus was claiming deity for Himself. Jesus was claiming to be God without a doubt. Jesus was not from Earth. He was from heaven. The heaven is His throne, and the earth is His footstool (Isa. 66:1).

*For this is good and acceptable in the sight of God
our Saviour.*

—1 Timothy 2:3

*For there are three that bear record in heaven, the
Father, the Word, and the Holy Ghost: and these
three are one.*

—1 John 5:7

Just as in John 1:1-3, 1 John 5:7 calls Jesus the Word. This scripture goes on to say that the three—the Father, the Word (Jesus) and the Holy Spirit are ONE.

John 1:14 says, "And the word was made flesh and dwelt among us." Jesus is the Word that was made a human being.

*And many other signs truly did Jesus in the pres-
ence of his disciples, which are not written in this
book: But these are written, that ye might believe
that Jesus is the Christ, the Son of God; and that
believing ye might have life through his name.*

—John 20:30-31

In the above text, the book of John was dedicated and committed to establishing the truth that Jesus was God—God the Son. It's says, "that ye might believe that Jesus is the Christ, the Son of God," God in the flesh.

> Go ye therefore, and teach all nations, baptizing them in the name of the Father, and of the Son, and of the Holy Ghost.
>
> —Matthew 28:19

In this verse, Jesus' name appears with God's in His commandment to baptize "in the name (singular) of the Father and of the Son and of the Holy Spirit" (parentheses mine).

Why did Jesus speak in the singular when commanding the baptism of new believers? In John 10:30, Jesus had clearly stated that He and the Father are one—one to the exclusion of another. Jesus was again claiming deity.

> And we know that the Son of God is come, and hath given us an understanding, that we may know him that is true, and we are in him that is true, even in his Son Jesus Christ. This is the true God, and eternal life.
>
> —1 John 5:20

This verse calls Jesus **"the true God and eternal life."** Titus 2:13 calls Jesus **"the great God and our Saviour."** A mathematical equation of these two scriptures would be: **Jesus = True God = Eternal Life = Great God = Our Saviour.**

Jesus is the true God, eternal life, great God, and our Savior!

I believe no one can read all these scriptures without any form of bias or preconceived notion and not come up with the conclusion that Jesus is truly God.

The Amplified Bible says, "…This [Man] is the true God and Eternal life" (1 John 5:20). Which man? Jesus. Surely Jesus is the true God and eternal life.

> *I charge thee therefore before God, and the Lord Jesus Christ, who shall judge the quick and the dead at his appearing and his kingdom.*
> —2 Timothy 4:1

Jesus, who is God, shall judge the living and the dead. Final judgment is reserved for God alone, and since Jesus shall judge the living and the dead, then He's got to be God.

We will all one day stand before God. Yes, before Jesus, the Righteous Judge. None shall escape, living or dead. However, believers, of course, will not be receiving judgment for damnation or banishment to the lake of fire, but for the purpose of receiving rewards at the judgment seat of Christ (Romans 14:10; 2 Corinthians 5:10). The unbelievers will appear before the white throne judgment (Rev. 20:11).

> *And he saw that there was no man, and wondered that there was no intercessor: therefore his arm brought salvation unto him; and his righteousness, it sustained him.*
> —Isaiah 59:16

This verse shows that no man could right the wrong that mankind brought unto themselves and the earth. Therefore, the

Lord fixed the problem Himself by becoming a man and bearing our punishment, so we could be reconciled to God.

Jesus, God the Son, became a man to fix the mess by suffering for the sins of the entire world (Isa. 53:4-5), and as a result, we were brought back into good terms with God. Notice that the Lord did it Himself. God saw that there was no man who could, so He did it Himself.

> The voice of him that crieth in the wilderness,
> Prepare ye the way of the LORD, make straight in
> the desert a highway for our God.
> —Isaiah 40:3

Doubtless, John the Baptist was the fulfillment of this prophecy (John 1:23; Matt. 3:1-3; Mark 1:2-4; Luke 3:2-5). He applied this passage of scripture to Himself, which means He also knew this was John's instruction and reference.

He was to "prepare the way of the Lord, and make straight in the desert a highway for our GOD." It's very clear that this scripture is referring to John preparing a way for Jesus, and interestingly enough, it says that Jesus is the Lord and our God. This is emphasizing **the divinity of Jesus prior to His birth.** Jesus is our Lord and our God. He was God before He became a human, God at birth, God on the cross, God in the grave, God in His resurrection, and God in heaven. Jesus is God even today. He is the same (Heb. 13:8).

John the Baptist made a highway for our God, the Lord Jesus.

And whence is this to me, that the mother of my
Lord should come to me?

—Luke 1:43

The Greek word used here for *Lord* is *"kurios"* and usually refers to Jehovah God. In context, this word is used **sixteen other times in this chapter**, and in each case, it clearly refers to **God**. There is no doubt that Elizabeth, under the inspiration of the Holy Ghost, was referring to Jesus as Lord, in the highest sense of the word. This further proves the divinity of Jesus.

We already saw Mary rejoice in God, her Savior, and how the angels praised God for Christ the Savior. Additionally, here Mary's cousin, Elizabeth, called Mary the mother of her Lord, which is a reference to God. This could read "And whence is this to me that the mother of my **God** should come to me?"

Since Mary was the mother of GOD (Jesus), then surely Jesus was God manifest in the flesh (1 Tim. 3:16).

Death of Jesus

One day, I was reading the account of Jesus' death, and I realized some very unique and completely exclusive occurrences to His death. These happenings spoke volumes as I sat back and meditated on them.

I want to share what dawned on me. Let me also say that these unique occurrences spoke volumes to me in light of Jesus' deity. I hope you find these occurrences interesting and full of revelation.

And, behold, the veil of the temple was rent in
twain from the top to the bottom; and the earth

> *did quake, and the rocks rent; And the graves were opened; and many bodies of the saints which slept arose, And came out of the graves <u>after</u> his resurrection, and went into the holy city, and appeared unto many. Now when the centurion, and they that were with him, watching Jesus, saw the earthquake, and those things that were done, they feared greatly, saying, <u>Truly this was the Son of God</u>.*
>
> —Matthew 27:51-54 (underline mine)

1) Darkness was all over the land for three hours from 12pm to 3pm (Matt. 27:45).

2) The earth did quake, and the rocks rent.

3) The veil of the temple was rent in two from the top to the bottom.

4) Graves were opened, and many bodies of the saints who slept arose and came out of their graves after his resurrection and went into the holy city and appeared to many.

Darkness

It is quite unique that from the sixth hour, there was darkness over all the land up to the ninth hour. When Jesus was on the cross, He died in the ninth hour (3pm), but for three hours leading up to the time he died, there was darkness over all the land.

Wow! Many people had been crucified. Jesus wasn't the first one, yet there was darkness over all the land for three hours uniquely at His death.

Now, if you have lost someone before, you know that there was no darkness over all the land. Why did this happen? I would speculate that it's because Jesus wasn't just a *mere* man. Jesus wasn't a man only. Jesus was God in the flesh (1 Tim. 3:16), and at his physical death, His creation responded (see Matt. 27:54).

Luke 23:45 says that the sun darkened at the death of Jesus. I believe this happened because Jesus was God in the flesh, and I also believe that these occurrences are uniquely tied **only** to Jesus.

Veil of the Temple Torn

There was a veil or huge, long curtain from ceiling to floor and wall to wall that separated the holy of holies from the holy place in the temple. When Jesus died, this enormous curtain was torn in two, opening and giving access to the holy of holies from the rest of the temple.

There's no doubt that no one could have torn the veil in this manner. It was definitely God who rent (tore) the veil, and the time of the veil being torn corresponds exactly with the moment that Jesus died.

Hebrews 9:1-9 reveals that the veil separated the holy of holies, where God dwelled, from the rest of the temple. This signified that man was separated from God by sin (Isa. 59:1-2), and only the high priest was permitted to pass beyond this veil, but only once each year (Ex.30:10; Heb. 9:7), symbolizing Christ entering into Father God's presence for us to make atonement.

The veil being torn in two revealed that the sacrifice had been made and that there was no longer any separation between

God and man. Jesus tore the veil, that is to say His flesh (Heb. 10:20), in two and opened a new way to God through Himself.

You can see that this was unique to Jesus' death alone and not to any other man. No other time in history is it recorded that when someone died, these events took place. This was totally unique to Jesus' death. Jesus, the great God (Tit. 2:13) and the true God (1 John 5:20) tore the veil and opened the door for you and me.

The Earth Did Quake and the Rocks Rent

Another unique thing that took place at the death of Jesus on the cross was that the earth did quake. Why did the earth quake only at the death of Jesus and not at the death of others like Buddha, Krishna, Mohammed or anyone else that claimed divinity?

It seems clear that something was unique about Jesus. I believe the unique aspect was that creation reacted or responded to the death of its Creator, the LORD Jesus Christ.

Graves Opened

The graves of those that had died opened, and many of the saints who had died arose.

Notice that even at the death of Jesus, such power was released that death lost its grip on its captives. "O death, where *is* thy sting? O grave, where *is* thy victory?" (1 Cor. 15:55) Death is swallowed up in victory. Death can be threatening, but not to a believer.

At Jesus' death, graves opened, and the dead saints came alive again. These people may have died years before Jesus, but at His death, they came alive again and came out into the streets after His resurrection. And they were seen by many people.

What a miracle this was! I suppose many, many saints who were dead came alive. They were resurrected.

This must have left the whole city amazed at the power of Jesus and who He was. What an impact this left on the entire country. I believe it got some who doubted Jesus to think again. All these unique events opened the eyes of some to who Jesus was.

Jesus was not a "normal man." He was God in a physical body.

Having seen all these events—darkness, the rocks rent, the earth quake, the veil torn in two and the graves opened, the centurion and the people that were with him watching Jesus feared greatly, and said, "Truly this was the Son of God.

> Now when the centurion, and they that were with him, watching Jesus, saw the earthquake, and those things that were done, they feared greatly, saying, _Truly this was the Son of God_.
> —Matthew 27:54 (underline mine)

The Centurion and those who were with him acknowledged that Jesus was God after they had seen all these unique events.

Boy, they saw what they had never seen. They were terrified and full of wonder. They finally said that Jesus was God, indeed the Son of God.

Who Raised Jesus from the Dead?

Many people have never thought about this question. If Jesus was truly God, then did He raise Himself from the dead? We see scriptures that say the Holy Spirit did, God the Father did, and Jesus did. So we learn that the entire Trinity was at work in the resurrection of Jesus. And since Jesus was and is God, it's accurate to say that He raised Himself from the dead. This further proves that He was and is God or else He couldn't have raised Himself from the dead. Look at the scriptures below.

God:

And God hath both raised up the Lord, and will also raise up us by his own power.
>   —1 Corinthians 6:14

Spirit of God:

But if the Spirit of him that raised up Jesus from the dead dwell in you, he that raised up Christ from the dead shall also quicken your mortal bodies by his Spirit that dwelleth in you.
>   —Romans 8:11

For Christ also hath once suffered for sins, the just for the unjust, that he might bring us to God, being put to death in the flesh, but quickened by the Spirit.
>   —1 Peter 3:18

Jesus:

Therefore doth my Father love me, because I lay down my life, that I might take it again. No man taketh it from me, but I lay it down of myself. I have power to lay it down, and I have power to

*take it again. This commandment have I received
of my Father.*

—John 10:17-18

*Then answered the Jews and said unto him, What
sign showest thou unto us, seeing that thou doest
these things? Jesus answered and said unto them,
Destroy this temple, and in three days I will raise
it up.*

—John 2:18-19

God the Father:

*Paul, an apostle, (not of men, neither by man, but
by Jesus Christ, and God the Father, who raised
him from the dead.)*

—Galatians 1:1

*Therefore we are buried with him by baptism into
death: that like as Christ was raised up from the
dead by the glory of the Father, even so we also
should walk in newness of life.*

—Romans 6:4

Was Jesus, God, man or both? Jesus was and is God. He was
100% God and 100% man.

Receive Jesus as Your Savior

Deciding to receive Jesus Christ as your Lord and Savior is the most important decision you'll ever make! Nothing comes close to this decision; not your career and surely not your wife. It will change your life now and your eternal destiny. There is no decision that could be made that is like it. It would be very sad for me to teach you that Jesus was and is God and not give you an opportunity to repent and to receive Him into your heart as your God and Savior. Will you accept Him as God not just another good man like some believe and say?

God has promised, "If thou shalt confess with thy mouth the Lord Jesus, and shalt believe in thine heart that God hath raised him from the dead, thou shalt be saved. For with the heart man believeth unto righteousness; and with the mouth confession is made unto salvation…. For whosoever shall call upon the name of the Lord shall be saved" (Rom. 10:9-10, 13).

By His grace, God has already done everything and His part to provide for your salvation. Your part is simply to believe and receive. It is the easiest decision. This is a heart decision, not a head decision. Now is the acceptable time, today is the day of salvation (2 Cor. 6:2). Why wait?

Pray this prayer and mean it sincerely from your heart:

Jesus,

I confess that You are my Lord and Savior. I believe in my heart that God raised You from the dead. By faith in Your Word, I receive salvation, now. Thank You for saving me!

The very moment you commit your life to Jesus Christ, the truth of His Word instantly comes to pass in your spirit. Now that you're born again, you are brand new on the inside of you. God has created in you a new spirit and a new heart.

Receive the Baptism of the Holy Spirit

Living a Christian life is not just a difficult thing to do but an impossible thing. You need help. So, because it is impossible to live a victorious, Christian life without the Baptism of the Holy Spirit, the Lord wants to give you the supernatural power you need to live this new life. We receive power when we receive the baptism of the Holy Spirit (Acts 1:8).

It's simple as asking and receiving. When we ask for the Holy Spirit, the Lord will give Him to us (Luke 11:10, 13).

All you have to do is ask, believe, and receive!

Pray:

Father,

I recognize my need for Your power to live this new life. Please fill me with Your Holy Spirit. By faith, I receive Him right now! Thank You for baptizing me. Holy Spirit, You are welcome in my life.

Congratulations! Now you're filled with God's supernatural power. Some syllables from a language you don't recognize will rise up from your heart to your mouth (See 1 Cor. 14:14). Go ahead and speak those syllables. As you speak them out loud by faith, you're releasing God's power from within and building yourself up in the Spirit (See 1 Cor. 14: 4). You can do this whenever and wherever you like.

It doesn't really matter whether you felt anything or not when you prayed to receive the Lord and His Spirit. If you believed in your heart that you received, then God's Word promises that you received. "Therefore I say unto you, What things soever ye desire, when ye pray, believe that ye receive them, and ye shall have them" (Mark 11:24). God always honors His Word—believe it!

About the Author

Rich Kanyali was born in Kampala, Uganda, on June 2, 1987. He lived there until after high school when he received Christ into his heart. In Uganda, it's not automatic that most people go on to university, but God opened a door for Rich to go to India and pursue a Bachelor of Commerce (BCOM) at Garden City College in Bangalore, an affiliate of Bangalore University. After his graduation in 2010, he moved to the United States to pursue his MBA. However, financially, things fell apart, and he could not afford school as an international student. God spoke to him to go to Charis Bible College and prepare for the ministry that God had called him to.

He graduated in 2017 with a Masters in Biblical Studies (MBS) and a license to preach the gospel of Jesus Christ. He has been teaching and bringing godly insight to the Scriptures since 2008 when he was in India. He established his first Bible study group with a few students at Garden City College. The group grew, and he later turned it over to another leader, whom he had raised up. He has been establishing groups and teaching God's Word!

He was also an ordained teacher and leader at his local church in India, tasked with leading and teaching the Adult Sunday School. He is a seasoned student of the Word and a teacher by gifting and calling. Rich's passion is to teach God's Word to the body of Christ with a greater emphasis on grace, faith, and making disciples, which in return will quickly turn the world right side up for King Jesus!

He is married to his lovely wife Joanna, and they have a beautiful daughter named Shalom.